DISASTER AT MOSCOW

DISASTER AT MOSCOW: VON BOCK'S CAMPAIGNS 1941-1942

BY ALFRED TURNEY

CASSELL · LONDON

CASSELL & COMPANY LTD.
35 Red Lion Square, London, WC1
Melbourne, Sydney, Toronto
Johannesburg, Auckland

First published in Great Britain 1971

I.S.B.N. 0 304 93668 5

Excerpts from the following works are used by permission:
Paul Carell, *Hitler's War on Russia (Hitler Moves East: 1941–1943)*,
tr. by E. Osers. London: George G. Harrap & Co. Ltd., 1964.
Heinz Guderian, *Erinnerungen eines Soldaten*. Heidelberg: Kurt
Vornwinckel Verlag, 1951.
Walter Warlimont, *Im Hauptquartier der deutschen Wehrmacht:
1939–1945*. Frankfurt: Athenäum Verlag, 1962.
John W. Wheeler-Bennett, *The Nemesis of Power: The German
Army in Politics—1918–1945*. London: Macmillan & Co. Ltd., 1953.

Printed Offset Litho in Great Britain by
Cox & Wyman Ltd., London, Fakenham and Reading
F.770

TO SARAH AND MIA

ACKNOWLEDGMENTS

I AM DEEPLY INDEBTED TO NUMEROUS persons in the preparation of this study. To Mr. Robert Wolfe and Mr. Richard Bauer, German Records Section, U.S. National Archives, Washington, D.C., I owe a special note of thanks for help in procuring an original copy of Field Marshal Fedor von Bock's war diary, photographs, and other materials.

Colonel Dr. R. Stahl, German Federal Archives, Coblenz, and Professor Dr. H. Krausnick, *Institut für Zeitgeschichte,* Munich, furnished valuable information pertaining to the records and registries of Field Marshal von Bock's military commands during the Second World War.

I wish to express gratitude to the Zimmerman Library, University of New Mexico, Albuquerque, for assistance in the procurement of German military records and documents. These materials were indispensable to this study.

The professional assistance and moral encouragement of Dr. Gunther E. Rothenberg, Professor of History, University of New Mexico, are gratefully acknowledged. Mrs. Olive Knox, Department of History, University of New Mexico, was always considerate and helpful during the many hours of research that went into the writing of this book.

The personal sources listed in the bibliography are the result of countless discussions and interviews with former officers and enlisted men of the German Wehrmacht, with whom I was in official and social contact as a military intelligence officer in the U.S. Army for many years after the Second World War. It was during this period, when I lived as a military officer of a foreign nation among the German people, that I conceived the idea for this narrative. It is not possible to thank individually each person named in the bibliography, but each one of them who may possibly read these lines will know that he or she contributed in no small part to whatever value this narrative may have.

Finally, I wish to say to my wife Sarah, "Thank you, dear." Without her help, both spiritual and material, this study would not have been possible.

TABLE OF CONTENTS

LIST OF ILLUSTRATIONS

MAPS AND DIAGRAMS

PHOTOGRAPHS

FIELD MARSHAL FEDOR VON BOCK

Commanded Army Group North in the Polish campaign, 1939; Army Group B in the conquest of Western Europe, 1940; Army Group Center in Russia, June-December 1941; dismissed by Hitler when Army Group floundered at gates of Moscow, December 1941; recalled to command Army Group South, January 1942; again dismissed by Hitler, July 1942.

FIELD MARSHAL WALTHER VON BRAUCHITSCH

Commander-in-Chief of German Army, 1938-41. Suffered heart attack, November 1941; dismissed when office of Commander-in-Chief assumed by Hitler, December 1941; lived in retirement until death, 1946.

COLONEL GENERAL HEINZ GUDERIAN

Commanded armored spearheads in Polish and Western European campaigns; dismissed by Hitler, December 1941; recalled a year later to rejuvenate *Panzerkorps;* served as Chief of General Staff in late months of war; wrote memoirs after war; died in retirement, 1954.

COLONEL GENERAL FRANZ HALDER

Chief of General Staff, 1938-42. Dismissed by Hitler after repeated disagreements over strategy and tactics; wrote memoirs, *Hitler as Warlord;* maintained voluminous diary of wartime activities (see Annotated Bibliography).

ADOLF HITLER

Führer of the Third Reich; modern history's greatest demagogue and perhaps the last of the great military conquerors.

COLONEL GENERAL ERIC HOEPNER

Expert in armored tactics; commanded tank army in Russian campaign; dismissed in disgrace by Hitler for alleged insubordination; implicated in July 1944 plot to kill Hitler; executed, August 1944.

COLONEL GENERAL HERMANN HOTH

Commanded one of tank armies that spearheaded the drive to Moscow, 1941; to Stalingrad, 1942; retired due to illness, 1943; wrote memoirs after war.

FIELD MARSHAL WILHELM KEITEL
Chief of Staff of Armed Forces High Command, 1938-45; known as Hitler's right-hand man; tried by International Military Tribunal, Nürnberg, convicted and executed, 1946.

FIELD MARSHAL ALBERT KESSELRING
Air Force officer, commanded Air Fleet 2 in invasion of Russia; later commander of all German forces in Italy; wrote memoirs after war; tried and convicted for "war crimes"; served abbreviated sentence; died, 1961.

FIELD MARSHAL GÜNTHER VON KLUGE
Commanded Fourth Army of Bock's Army Group Center in Russian campaign; replaced Bock as commander of Army Group Center, December 1941; implicated in July 1944 plot to kill Hitler; committed suicide in France, August 1944.

FIELD MARSHAL WILHELM LIST
Commanded Army Group B (later Bock's Army Group Center), fall of 1940; later commander in Balkans; after war, held in prison by Yugoslavs, where he died.

LIEUTENANT GENERAL RUDOLF SCHMUNDT
Hitler's aide-de-camp; killed when bomb exploded in plot to kill Hitler, July 1944.

COLONEL GENERAL ADOLF STRAUSS
Commander of Ninth Army in Bock's Army Group Center in Russian campaign, 1941; dismissed after failure at Moscow; retired due to illness, 1943.

COLONEL GENERAL MAXIMILIAN FREIHERR VON WEICHS
Commander of Second Army assigned to Bock's Army Group Center in Russian campaign, 1941; replaced Bock as commander of Army Group South in Southern Russia, July 1942.

MARSHAL GREGORI K. ZHUKOV (OF THE SOVIET UNION)
Commander of Russian troops which counterattacked at Moscow, December 1941; Zhukov's troops entered Berlin, 1945.

O N E   O F   T H E   I R O N I E S   I N   T H E history of the Second World War is that at almost the exact moment when the Germans conceded failure at Moscow in December 1941, the Japanese attacked United States naval and military installations at Pearl Harbor and in the Philippine Islands. The Japanese attack brought America and her enormous resources into the war on the side of Great Britain and Soviet Russia and enlarged the war to global proportions. The Japanese attack on United States territory also had one other momentous result. It momentarily diverted the attention of the Western world from the deadly drama that was being enacted at the gates of Moscow. This explains in part why there is surprisingly little literature in the Western world about the Battle of Moscow. There is practically none at all about Fedor von Bock, the individual who, aside perhaps from Adolf Hitler, played the most decisive role in this major turning point of the Second World War.

Why was the Battle of Moscow so decisive? How was it that the German military forces so nearly succeeded—then failed? The answers to these questions lie in the complex issues of military strategy and tactics that confronted Hitler in the first victorious years of the war. Since September 1939, the German military forces had conquered Poland, Denmark, Norway, the Low Countries, and France and had driven the British off the European Continent. The German Army's blitzkrieg tactics, which involved coordinated air, infantry, and armored thrusts deep into enemy territory, had dismayed Germany's enemies and had exceeded the wildest dreams of the German military officers who were responsible for executing this new concept of warfare. Germany's military victories in 1939 and 1940 had given her armed forces an image of invincibility.

In the summer of 1940 German armed might stood supreme in Western and Central Europe. But Hitler, like Napoleon 130 years earlier, was confronted with the specter of an undefeated Great Britain. Hitler had never planned to invade Great Britain; he confidently—but erroneously—believed that the British would come to terms with him, once German hegemony had been established over Western Europe. Thus, while carrying out a rather half-hearted attempt to subdue the British people by air power, Hitler made the strategic decision to turn eastward against the Soviet Union, with its great land mass, huge population, and unlimited natural resources.

The decision to annihilate the Soviet Union was not made on the spur of the moment. Hitler was a determined exponent of the philosophy of geopolitics, which had been set forth several decades earlier by a number of German intellectuals. The geopolitical philosophy stated, in essence, that Russia was the heartland of the Euro-Asian continent, and that the nation that ruled Russia ruled the world. Moreover, Hitler had used the natural fear of Russian Communism, or Bolshevism, among the German aristocratic and industrial classes as a stepping stone in his rise to power. From the beginning of a political career that carried him to the pinnacle of power, Hitler had vowed to launch a crusade against Bolshevism at the earliest opportunity. With respect to his announced intention of destroying Bolshevism, Hitler had the general support of the Prussian Junkers and other land-owning aristocracy and of the militarists, of which Fedor von Bock was a member.

Thus it would appear that Hitler's decision to invade the Soviet Union in 1941 was fundamentally and politically sound, notwithstanding all subsequent apologia by German generals after the war. There remained only the implementation of the decision. This the German Armed Forces, after the fall of France in June 1940, prepared almost leisurely to do. During the eight-month period between August 1940 and April 1941, the German Armed Forces concentrated on Germany's eastern borders the most powerful military force ever assembled in modern history. Standing among the vanguard of this great force was one of Germany's foremost militarists, Field Marshal Fedor von Bock, in whom Hitler placed implicit trust, often against the advice of his closest associates.

Having made the strategic decision to attack and destroy the Soviet Union, Hitler then proceeded to make a series of fatal errors in its implementation. The first of these was the postponement of the invasion for six weeks, to settle the suddenly developing Balkan crisis by armed force. It is noteworthy that von Bock protested the postponement on the soldierly grounds that it adversely affected the morale of his troops. Some historians and students of the period have claimed that the German armies were sufficiently powerful to overrun the Balkans without materially affecting preparations for the campaign in Russia. The interpretation, however, that postponing the invasion of the Soviet Union cost final victory for Germany would appear to be farfetched.

Once the invasion began on 22 June 1941, the inadequate communications and road networks in the Soviet Union slowed down the German armored, motorized, and infantry divisions far more effectively than did the Russian defenders and threw the invasion timetable off schedule on practically the first day. This loss of time and the large elements of the Red Army that managed to escape the German armored encirclements presented Hitler and the German Armed Forces with a dilemma.

In an effort to solve the dilemma, Hitler made his second fatal error. In August 1941 he halted the headlong advance to Moscow and directed the German forces to encircle and destroy huge concentrations of Russian forces in the Ukraine. It is again noteworthy that von Bock bitterly protested this change in tactical operations. Bock's reasons for protesting the change were military, but in so doing he began to incur Hitler's distrust.

With the conclusion of the Battle of Kiev in September 1941, which proved to be a monumental but indecisive tactical victory, Hitler was again confronted with the necessity to decide how to continue the campaign. The Russian summer was drawing to a close, and the beginning of the autumn rainy season just weeks away. Should the German armies go on to Moscow, less than 200 miles distant? How effective would Russian resistance be? Had the Russians been given time to erect fortifications and lines of defense in front of their capital?

In his decision to renew the assault on Moscow and to capture the city before the onset of winter, Hitler was strongly influenced by von Bock. To Bock a continuation of the attack on Moscow was a matter of professional pride and military achievement. He had sat for two months, from the end of July to the end of September, awaiting this grand opportunity to march into the Soviet Russian capital. He did not intend to forego it.

Soon after the final assault on Moscow began, the rains came and von Bock's forces floundered in the mud. Even so, they probably could have reached Moscow had von Bock been able to resist the temptation to destroy almost a million Russian soldiers trapped at Bryansk and at Vyasma. This was perhaps von Bock's most serious error of the German campaigns in Russia.

By the time his men had extricated themselves from the Bryansk-Vyasma battles, the Russian winter had come, and it literally froze Bock's Army Group Center to a standstill within sight of Moscow. Now it was von Bock who faced a dreadful alternative: either he continued the attack, or he and his huge force faced disaster in the snow and ice. At this point, the Army High Command, with Hitler's approval, decided to place the responsibility for a continuation or a cancellation of the attack directly on Bock. Naturally, Bock chose to attack, but by then it was too late. The German forces could not overcome the handicaps of nature, the breakdown of their own supply system, and the dogged resistance of the Russian defenders.

The German military forces suffered their first, and most serious, setback of the Second World War.

It is mere conjecture to dwell upon the war's outcome if von Bock's forces had succeeded in capturing Moscow. It is fairly certain that the Soviet Russian government would have continued to fight against the German invaders from the Russian hinterland. Indeed, the original plan for the invasion, Operation *Barbarossa,* envisioned this contingency by providing for an enormous military patrol force of sixty divisions, or about a million men, extending from the shores of the Barents Sea in the north to the Afghanistan borders in the south. Yet the German conquest of Moscow in August or September or October of 1941, at a time when Bock's forces still possessed sufficient strength to hold the city, would have inflicted both a psychological and military defeat upon the Russians, the effects of which cannot be assessed.

Conversely, the German failure at Moscow had adverse effects on German morale, both at home and on the thousands of frozen German soldiers who were left stranded in the snow on the approaches to the city. Most significantly, the failure resulted in Hitler's assumption of operational command of the German Army, an event that sounded the death knell for German professional militarism.

Perhaps the most conservative of all the professional militarists during the Second World War was Fedor von Bock. His character was dominated by a mixture of national pride, political disinterest, patriotic dedication, and, most importantly, a haughty awareness of his high military position. The latter trait manifested itself in a stubborn capacity to act independently and without regard to any mitigating factor from below or above that might tend to divert him from the fulfillment of his obligation as a Prussian-German soldier.

Unlike many other German generals, even among the Prussian aristocratic class, von Bock was impassive and inured to hardship. He was austere in his own living habits, and he expected austerity in others. His compassion for the human suffering and misery of his soldiers on the battlefield extended only to the degree that these things prevented the soldiers from accomplishing their mission. It seems not to have occurred to Bock that his military commands should not be obeyed. When it came to the execution of military operations, Bock was apparently a man who could set aside ordinary human emotions. Statements by subordinate commanders that Bock was a difficult man to serve and the nicknames given him, such as the "Holy Fire" and *Der Sterber* (fatalist), attest to this fact.

Perhaps the most curious aspect of all was the strange relationship between Hitler and von Bock. No two men could have been farther apart in character and personality. Yet Hitler instinctively trusted von Bock to the extent that he defended him against his detractors. After the disaster at Moscow, Hitler felt impelled to recall von Bock to duty and to charge him with the responsibility for yet another huge field command. Even after Hitler and Bock came to a final parting of the ways in July 1942, Hitler regarded

Bock's military reputation as worthy of a great hoax, which he imposed upon Germany and, for a short time, the world.

The institution of Prussian militarism, which produced men like Field Marshal von Bock, disappeared with the complete political, social, economic, and military collapse of the Nazi German state in 1945. Where the Prussian Junkers once ruled their estates and their ancient cities with iron-handed discipline stand today the collective farms and other socialist institutions of two Communist states, East Germany and Poland.

There is at present no indication that Prussian militarism will ever again be a formidable force in Europe, at least for generations to come. In this respect, it seems more than a coincidence that Fedor von Bock's death by violent means in the closing days of the Second World War occurred almost simultaneously with the violent death of Prussian aristocratic militarism.

DISASTER AT MOSCOW:

VON BOCK'S CAMPAIGNS, 1941-42

I. FROM LIEUTENANT TO FIELD MARSHAL:
THE "HOLY FIRE OF KÜSTRIN"

FEDOR VON BOCK

was born on 3 December 1880 in Küstrin, an ancient fortress city on the banks of the Oder River about fifty miles east of Berlin. A Prussian Protestant aristocrat, he was given at birth the full name of Moritz Albrecht Franz Friedrich Fedor.

Bock's military heritage is traceable to the time of the early Hohenzollerns. His great-grandfather fought in the armies of Frederick the Great; his grandfather was an officer in the Prussian Army at Jena. Bock's father, General Karl Moritz von Bock, commanded a division in the Franco-Prussian War of 1870-71 and was decorated for bravery at Sedan. Bock's mother, Olga Helene Franszika Freifrau von Falkenhayn von Bock, was of both German and Russian aristocratic heritage. On his mother's side, Bock was distantly related to the Falkenhayn military family, whose most notable figure, General Erich von Falkenhayn, directed the fortunes of the Imperial German Armies for two years (1914-16) in the First World War.[1]

Bock grew up in the stern, austere environment of a Prussian Junker. Ten years before his birth, Otto von Bismarck had founded the German Empire, literally hammering out the new German Reich on the anvil of wars and shrewd diplomacy.

When Bock was eight his parents sent him to Berlin to be educated at the Potsdam and Gross Lichterfelde military academies. Here Bock followed the strict, disciplined routine of a Prussian military cadet. His education was, however, well rounded and preferential, for he became adept in such academic subjects as modern languages, mathematics, and history. Bock spoke French fluently and English and Russian to a fair degree.

Above all else, Bock's educational development emphasized Prussian militarism. The army, the most powerful single institution in the Second Reich, reveled in its confirmed status as a state within a state. This concept was reflected in the curricula of the military academies and Bock applied himself dutifully and diligently to his studies.

When Bismarck fell from power in 1890, the Prussian Junkers emerged as the dominant influence in unified Germany. Traditionally, Prussia was a *"Soldaten- und Beamtenstaat,* a state of soldiers and bureaucracy, a state formed by and for war, a *Machtstaat* in which mechanical efficiency of the highest order became united with the . . . notions of political obedience and obligations. . . ."[2] In Prussia the profession of arms was the highest calling a man could pursue.

This tradition influenced the development of young Bock's character. From an early age, under his father's tutelage, he became imbued with the concept of unquestioning loyalty to the state and dedication to the military profession. The new German Reich was the product of a series of victorious wars; Bock was taught that it was his life's obligation, as a professional military officer, to serve Prussia-Germany's further glorification. These early teachings were to remain with Bock throughout his life. They were to close his mind to every consideration except the most immediate consequences of his status as a soldier in the service of the Fatherland. In later years, when Bock was a field marshal in command of more than a million German soldiers, his earlier Prussian upbringing would override his extensive military training and would impel him to accede to Adolf

Hitler's instructions even when he knew those instructions were militarily impractical.

Yet Bock never became a National Socialist. Unlike some other professional military officers of the Third Reich, such as Werner von Blomberg, Walther von Reichenau, and Heinz Guderian, he never used the raised-hand Nazi salute; and there is evidence that he regarded the pompous trappings of the Nazis with some disdain. He considered himself to be above their rowdy political and propaganda machinations. It is alleged that in 1938, at an official reception at the Reich Chancellory, Hermann Göring, who along with Bock held the *Pour le Mérite,* approached Bock, saying that as coholders of Germany's highest military honor they could well be good friends. Bock gave Göring a cold stare and told him in no uncertain terms that the medals on their collars did not make them social equals.[3]

On the other hand, Bock regarded Hitler as the chief of state and supreme commander of the armed forces, and he refers to Hitler in almost reverent terms in his war diary. As a high commander during the Third Reich's early victories in the Second World War, Bock usually concluded his orders of the day to his soldiers with *Es lebe der Führer,* but not with the expression *Heil dem Führer* used by more Nazi-inclined commanders.[4]

In 1897, at the age of seventeen, Bock became an officer candidate in the Imperial Foot Guards Regiment at Potsdam. A year later, he received an officer's commission with an assignment to the same organization. Lieutenant Bock was now developing those physical and mental characteristics that would later carry him to the very top in the German military hierarchy. He was tall, thin, narrow-shouldered, ramrod straight. His sharp features, piercing green eyes, and thin-lipped expression gave him an emaciated, almost hungry appearance. He seldom smiled; his humor was dry and cynical. His arrogant, aloof manner, unbending military bearing and cold absorption in his profession foretold a determination, industry, and nerveless physical courage for which war correspondents would give him the awesome title of "master of the total assault," as he ordered hundreds of thousands of Germany's finest young men into the terrifying maw that was the final battle for Moscow in late 1941.[5]

Bock was not a brilliant theoretician, but his determination to succeed more than made up for a lack of brilliance. During the late 1920s and early 1930s, when Bock ranked among the highest officers in the German *Reichswehr*, he was sometimes invited to address graduating cadets at his alma mater. He was a fiery lecturer, and his theme was always that the greatest glory that could come to the German soldier was to die on the battlefield for the Fatherland. For these fiery, fanatical exhortations, Bock was given the title "Holy Fire of Küstrin."[6]

During the years following his entry into the commissioned ranks of the army, Bock followed the happy routine of a young professional officer in a peaceful, prospering Germany. In October 1905, he married Mally von Reichenbach, a young Prussian noblewoman whom he had met in Berlin. Bock and his bride took their marriage vows at a traditionally colorful military wedding at the Potsdam garrison. In 1907, a daughter was born to this marriage.[7]

In 1906 Bock attended the War Academy in Berlin. After a year's intensive study in the art and science of war, he joined the elite ranks of the General Staff. In the General Staff's Deployment Section, Bock learned about the intricate workings of the German military organization. He joined the super-patriotic Army League and became a close associate of other young German officers, such as Walther von Brauchitsch, Franz Halder, and Gerd von Rundstedt, with whom some thirty years later he would play a leading role in the Second World War.

In 1910 tragedy struck Bock's personal life. His young wife died after a sudden brief illness.[8]

When the First World War erupted all over Europe in 1914, Bock was assigned as divisional staff officer in Bavarian Crown Prince von Rupprecht's army group on the Western Front. For the next two years he took part in planning Rupprecht's campaigns, including the bloody, indecisive Battle of Verdun (February–November 1916). Captain von Bock eventually tired of the tenacious, frustrating routine of military staff duty. It is probable that his desire for personal advancement became an overriding consideration. At any rate, he requested in 1917 to be assigned to a field command. At first his requests were ignored, but with the persistence that would characterize Bock's long military career he managed to obtain an audience with von Rupprecht himself. He must have impressed the Crown Prince, for shortly thereafter Bock became commander of an infantry battalion and was promoted to major.[9]

He led his battalion in the Somme and Cambrai campaigns, but without conspicuous success. His battalion suffered more than the usual heavy losses that accompanied infantry assaults in the First World War and at one time during the campaigns of 1918 it was reduced to less than thirty percent of its original manpower strength. Bock's efforts, however, earned for him in 1917 the *Pour le Mérite* and in 1918 he received the Order of Hohenzollern, Imperial Germany's second highest military honor.

The role that Bock played in the last months of the First World War is strange and obfuscated. As Germany approached collapse, Bock became concerned about the Hohenzollern monarchy's continued existence. In the despairing days of early November 1918, he accompanied Crown Prince von Rupprecht to Berlin to beg William II not to abdicate the throne.[10] The mission was unsuccessful. Nevertheless, Bock remained strongly pro-monarchist, and during the hectic revolutionary days following Germany's surrender, his battalion, which was still part of the regular army, helped to suppress leftist uprisings in Berlin. It seems that Bock developed during this time a strong contempt for the German Weimar Republic, and though he elected to remain uninvolved in the abortive attempts by right-wingers to restore the monarchy, there was little doubt as to where his sympathies lay. The reasons for this are not too obscure. Bock was a Prussian militarist, his creed was that of a stern disciplinarian, and the democratic character of the Weimar Republic was distasteful to him.

The Treaty of Rapallo, signed in 1922 between the Soviet Russian regime and the struggling German Weimar Republic, exerted a direct influence upon Bock's military career. Shortly after the treaty was signed, Bock received a promotion to lieutenant colonel and went secretly to Soviet Russia. There he played a prominent role in the organization and training of the *Schwarze Reichswehr*.[11]

By early 1924 Bock was back in Berlin, and for the next three years he was assigned to the Troop Office, the subterfuge substitute for the prohibited General Staff. Until 1928, he was a staff officer at the Troop Office; this four-year period would be his last tenure as a staff officer. From then on, he would be a field commander. In late 1928 he moved to Frankfurt an der Oder to take command of the 1st Cavalry Regiment, the organization that would later form the nucleus of the Wehrmacht's cavalry forces in the Second World War.

Bock's rise in rank and authority was gradual but steady. The year 1930 found him in Stettin as commander of the 1st Infantry Division. He remained in command of this hardline old Prussian unit for about a year. When the German Army underwent a reorganization in 1931, Bock became commander of a military district and was promoted to lieutenant general. He held this command during the economic depression and political upheavals in Germany of the early 1930s.

Although little is known of Bock's immediate reaction to Hitler's appointment to the German chancellorship in early 1933, it is certain that he played no direct part in this fateful event. Conservative Prussian militarist that he was, Bock regarded Hitler's National Socialists and their roughhouse tactics with a jaundiced eye. Yet his very conservatism and devotion to the military profession tended to isolate Bock from political affairs. The chancellorship was a political office; its functions and who held it concerned Bock only insofar as they affected Germany's military future. Hitler promised fame and glory for Germany and for the German military organization. Bock wanted to share in this fame and glory; therefore, he accepted Hitler in this light.

In April 1935, shortly after Hitler proclaimed military conscription and created the Wehrmacht, Bock assumed command of Army Group 3 at Dresden. Rearmament and reconstruction of the German military machine now became of utmost importance. It was "pushed with great haste —and indeed there was, in some ways, a war atmosphere in Germany."[12] The Third Reich's entire economic policy was geared to military expansion. Heavy industries began once more, as in the years before and during the First World War, to produce war materiel and weapons. New barracks, garrisons, airfields, military training sites, and firing ranges were laid out and built at a rapid pace. And General von Bock, from his vantage point as an army group commander in the picturesque city of Dresden, reveled in all the new, hectic military activity: the processing of recruits, the arrival of new arms and equipment, the sharp commands of veteran noncommissioned officers resounding across the drill grounds, and the pomp and pageantry of ceremonial parades and formal troop inspections. These things represented for Bock the ultimate in his life's calling; he was, first and last, a Prussian-German soldier.

In mid-1937 Bock transferred to Berlin to assume command of Army Group 1, which comprised some of the German Army's elite troops. Along with this transfer he received a promotion to colonel general. Bock was now the army's third highest officer, ranking in seniority next to the Commander-in-Chief, Colonel General Werner Freiherr von Fritsch, and to the oldest active officer in terms of age and length of service, Colonel General Gerd von Rundstedt.[13]

Bock had met Hitler officially on several previous occasions. But now that his headquarters were in Berlin he came into more frequent contact with the Führer. There developed during the following months a strange relationship between the two men. It was a relationship based not upon mutual affection but upon a sort of mutual acceptance. Hitler, the self-willed, megalomaniac leader of the Third Reich, impressed Bock with his charisma and dreams of Germany's future glory; Bock, the military professional, impressed Hitler with his soldierly arrogance and single-minded devotion to military matters. This relationship would survive troubled times during the early war years. In his unfathomable way, Hitler would condescend to Bock even while distrusting the entire German Officers Corps. And Bock, in his capacity of a field marshal commanding an army group, would display a blind loyalty to Hitler even while criticizing and quarreling with high army leadership to the point of outright insubordination.

There may have been several reasons for the strange relationship that developed between Hitler and von Bock. But perhaps the most important one concerned Hitler's struggle in 1937-38 with the Officers Corps for ultimate control of Germany's destiny. In this struggle Bock survived such fateful events as the Blomberg-Fritsch crisis; the break between Hitler and the Chief of the General Staff, Colonel General Ludwig Beck, and the latter's resignation; the dismissal of several high-ranking officers; and Hitler's emergence as Supreme Commander of the German Armed Forces. Bock did this by remaining publicly aloof and noncommittal during the crises, and by steadfastly refusing to involve himself in an anti-Hitler conspiracy. Although he was approached in utmost secrecy several times during the prewar years and immediately following the war's outbreak regarding his tentative position in such a conspiracy, Bock dismissed all such overtures with a contemptuous "Nonsense!"[14]

While the struggle between Hitler and the officers still seethed, Bock was selected to command the army contingents that marched into Austria during the *Anschluss* of March 1938. Whether or not Hitler personally made the selection or merely approved it is not entirely clear. The march, though peaceful, was the most severe test yet of the newly established motorized and armored divisions. As the units advanced into Austria from the German border there were numerous mechanical breakdowns and considerable confusion and frustrating delays in the march columns. This displeased the outspoken von Bock to the extent that an enmity arose between him and the commander of the 2nd Panzer Division, Major General Heinz Guderian, who led the march. This enmity would carry into the Second World War.[15]

After the Austrian *Anschluss,* Bock returned to Berlin as commander of Army Group 1. He took no active part in the bloodless conquest of the Sudetenland in September 1938, nor in the occupation of Czechoslovakia in the spring of the following year.

In October 1938 von Rundstedt, who had been dismissed from command earlier in the year, announced his retirement. Bock became the German Army's senior ranking officer. There is evidence that Bock then expected to be appointed commander-in-chief.[16] This appointment did not materialize and though Bock remained, as always, loyal to Hitler, he became increasingly critical of policies at German High Command.

Early in 1939 Hitler decided definitely that the long-standing dispute between Germany and Poland must be resolved by military force. As a consequence of this decision, the Wehrmacht intensified its preparations for actual warfare. Using summer maneuvers as a disguise, the German Army began to concentrate on the Polish border. By 25 August 1939 von Bock was in command of Army Group North whose mission was to erase the Polish Corridor and then to destroy Polish forces north of the Weichsel River.

After the successful blitzkrieg in Poland, Bock returned to Berlin and became involved with preparations for the forthcoming campaign in the West. His pattern of expressing discontent during the period of the "Phony War" permeated various aspects of the operations that affected his army group. On one occasion he confided to his diary: "Why does not Brauchitsch permit me more freedom of movement?"[17]

On another occasion Bock granted an interview to the High Command Chief Propaganda Officer, Colonel Hesse. Bock expressed his views regarding propaganda and the Western campaign:

The most effective propaganda is to present openly and clearly the indisputable ethical reasons for the growth and development of the Prussian-German Armies and why they are being utilized in this fashion (attack in the West). . . . Our propaganda effort should also make clear that we are inviting our defeated enemies to cooperate with us in the grand Prussian-German plan. Only if this is done does propaganda come to life, and all concerned will hold their breath in awe and anticipation. I fear, however, that the High Command has neither the authority nor the ability to implement such propaganda. . . .[18]

After numerous postponements the German Army attacked France, Belgium, and Holland on 10 May 1940. In the Western campaign Bock's Army Group B was given a diversionary mission. Von Rundstedt, who had been recalled to duty from retirement shortly before the outbreak of war, commanded Army Group A and bore the brunt of the main attack. Bock's forces attacked the weaker Dutch and Belgian troops to distract the French and English forces from the main attack at Sedan. If his pride was injured because of his secondary mission in the Western campaign, it was restored somewhat when he himself was authorized to negotiate the surrender of Belgium's King Leopold and his army in late May 1940.[19] Nonetheless, as the German forces sped through France and reached the Atlantic Coast, Bock was among the most vehement opponents of the controversial decision to halt the advance at Dunkirk.

Still Bock was naturally well pleased with the Wehrmacht's spectacular successes in Western Europe. Following France's surrender and her signing of an armistice on 24 June 1940, Army Group B set up headquarters in Paris, and Bock established residence in a Paris hotel. During the next weeks, he made frequent trips to Berlin, traveling sometimes via Brussels and sometimes directly between Paris and the German capital.

For the time being, he applied himself to the task of administering the military occupation of France, but except for a brief show of concern over the plight of French refugees and displaced civilians, he seems to have regarded this task far less seriously than the mission of conquering the French state by military force.

On 26 June the German High Command ordered that its field forces in France be drastically reduced and reorganized for military occupation duties. When Bock received this order, he displayed his usual disregard for political matters and his arrogant cynicism for the "higher-ups." Although Bock seems to have thought that England would soon capitulate, the future prosecution of the war did not, for the moment, concern him. His comment was:

Today I received orders concerning reorganization of the army group. Fifteen divisions will be transferred to East Prussia to display a friendly but firm attitude towards the Russians. Some of my divisions will be deactivated; the number of motorized and panzer divisions will be substantially increased in the homeland. The remainder of my army group stays in France. Thus with two very much weakened armies I am given the mission of securing the Atlantic coastline from Brest to the Spanish border. I wonder if they think the coast is going to run away, or if the demarcation line will be stolen![20]

A few days later, Bock conferred with Halder about the care of the millions of French refugees left homeless and destitute by the war. In definite terms, he stated that the refugees should be allowed to return unmolested to their homes and that since the French harvest was for the most part lost for the season, French farmers should be assisted in providing food for themselves and their families. Past experience, Bock stated to Halder, showed that the situation returned more quickly to normal when people were allowed to look after themselves and when they realized that relief was forthcoming. Bock complained that during the campaign he had been hindered by Army High Command in his intention to rehabilitate the refugees. Moreover it was both an advantage to the occupation forces as well as an act of humanitarianism to tackle the problem immediately.

Halder agreed in substance but told Bock that the refugee

and food problem was more acute in the cities than on the farms. Bock replied: "Well, I would like to have more freedom in dealing with the matter and I think it is important to release the French prisoners immediately, so that they can return to their homes and places of work."[21]

Halder agreed with this, too, but explained that providing transportation for the refugees and prisoners would overtax the army's transportation capabilities. Bock brushed this aside and stated that as long as Army High Command gave him the authority he would deal with the transportation problem; in fact, he would give high priority to the whole matter of rehabilitation in France.

Bock did not mention the matter again, though he apparently acted with some alacrity to resolve it. He was thwarted in whatever intention he may have had to secure the release of French prisoners of war. Almost two million Frenchmen would remain in German camps until they were released by advancing Allied forces in the last months of the war. Humanitarianism no doubt entered.Bock's mind, but he was as much concerned with facilitating the task of occupation as he was with helping French refugees.

The summer of 1940 was a memorable time for Bock, probably the most memorable of his long military career. On 18 July, he traveled to Berlin and on the next day, along with the other high officers of the Wehrmacht, he heard Hitler address the Reichstag. During the speech Hitler thanked the Wehrmacht for its successful accomplishments; afterward the generals and admirals gathered at a reception given for them by Hitler. At the reception Bock received the baton of General Field Marshal. Bock made no mention of the promotion, but in typical, devoted fashion he remarked that as a result of "Hitler's warm words of gratitude the army has now come into its full right."[22]

During the remainder of July and throughout August Bock alternated his time between his headquarters in Paris and his home in Berlin. On one occasion, 14 August, he saw Hitler again at a luncheon that a number of high officers also attended and heard him speak about the necessity for closer relations between the German people and the German Army, so that the latter will "eventually come to recognize and acknowledge the great philosophy of National Socialism."[23]

Hitler brought up the subject of German-Russian relations and, according to Bock, jovially suggested that one very competent German general should be sent to Russia as an undercover agent to keep the Russians quiet. In actuality, Hitler had already decided to attack the Soviet Union, but von Bock was apparently unaware of the decision.

The pleasant days of a Parisian summer and leisurely travel were soon to end. On the last day of August, Bock's headquarters received a preparatory order from Army High Command, stating that within the next few days Army Group B was to be transferred to East Prussia. Von Kluge's Fourth Army would form the vanguard of the transfer; it was to be followed by a number of corps and divisional staffs and finally by Bock's headquarters.[24]

Bock spent the next day or so in speculation about this new move. He telegraphed von Brauchitsch for clarification of Army High Command's instructions but received academic replies. He visited his colleague and subordinate army commander, von Kluge, and discussed the matter. And he confided to his diary: "What mission I will have in East Prussia and what will develop there I do not as yet know. . . . Probably they want me to act as a kind of scarecrow for the Russians."[25]

On 11 September 1940, Bock relinquished command of his occupation area in France to Field Marshal Ritter von Leeb and proceeded to Berlin. The "Holy Fire of Küstrin" would never see Paris again.

1. *Current Biography* (New York, 1942), p. 62.

2. Koppel S. Pinson, *Modern Germany* (New York, 1966), p. 8.

3. William Bayles, "General von Bock," *American Mercury,* vol. LV, no. 223 (New York, August 1941), p. 184.

4. See *Generalfeldmarschall von Bock Kriegstagebuch: Mai 1939–Mai 1945,* Microfilm T-84 (Washington, D.C.: U.S. National Archives, n.d.). Hereafter cited as von Bock KTB.

5. Bayles, p. 183.   6. *Ibid.,* p. 186.

7. *Current Biography,* p. 64.   8. *Ibid.,* p. 64.   9. p. 65.   10. p. 66.

11. The term refers to the Weimar Republic's secret army, sometimes referred to as *Arbeitskommandos,* or labor units. The *Schwarze Reichswehr* was formed in the early 1920s to circumvent the restriction placed on Germany's military forces by the Treaty of Versailles. The full story of Germany's secret rearmament still remains to be told; it is certain, however, that von Bock figured prominently in it. See Pinson, pp. 434–35; John W. Wheeler-Bennett, *The Nemesis of Power* (New York, 1964), pp. 92–94; Paul Carell, *Hitler Moves East: 1941-1943* (Boston, 1963), pp. 191-217; and personal sources (Annotated Bibliography, pp. 215-20).

12. T. L. Jarman, *The Rise and Fall of Nazi Germany* (New York, 1956), p. 176.

13. Telford Taylor, *Sword and Swastika* (New York, 1952), p. 274.

14. Von Bock KTB, 22 August 1939.

15. Heinz Guderian, *Erinnerungen eines Soldaten* (Heidelberg, 1951), pp. 42-48; von Bock KTB; and personal sources. Guderian states that von Bock became extremely angry because he, Guderian, ordered the German armored vehicles bedecked with flags and flowers during the advance into Austria. Von Bock apparently considered this a violation of strict military procedure.

16. Personal interview with Major General Anton Grasser, 1953.

17. Von Bock KTB, 8 September 1939.   18. *Ibid.,* 6 February 1940.

19. *Ibid.,* 27 May 1940.   20. 28 June 1940.   21. 4 July 1940.

22. 19 July 1940.   23. 14 August 1940.

24. Kurt von Tippelskirch, *Geschichte des Zweiten Weltkrieges* (Bonn, 1951), p. 199; Hans-Adolf Jacobsen (ed.), *Generaloberst Halder Kriegstagebuch,* vol. II (Stuttgart, 1963), p. 82 (hereafter cited as

Halder KTB); von Bock KTB, 31 August 1940. Tippelskirch states that von Bock's Army Group B, with elements of the Fourth, Twelfth, and Eighteenth armies, began to transfer to East Prussia in July 1940. Von Bock states in his war diary that transfer orders were not received until 30 August. Bock's statement is corroborated in Halder KTB.

25. Von Bock KTB, 31 August 1940.

WHEN FIELD MAR-

shal von Bock arrived in Berlin from Paris in September 1940, German troops had already begun to concentrate secretly in East Prussia and occupied Poland. Despite the fact that the English and, for that matter, the entire world anticipated a German attempt to invade England, the Wehrmacht had ordered a reduction of forces in the West. The reduction was carried out under cover of the more obvious preparations for the invasion of England (Operation *Sea Lion*). During the weeks following France's surrender, only infantry troops were involved in the transfer, for their presence in the East was easier to camouflage. Armored and motorized divisions, with their more aggressive character, remained temporarily in France, Belgium, and Holland, presumably to be employed as cross-channel invasion troops but in reality to provide deception for the eastern concentrations and to be transferred later under other pretexts.[1]

Naturally von Bock was aware that the Wehrmacht was shifting its strength from West to East. In late June 1940 while still in Paris he had transferred at Army High Command's direction fifteen infantry divisions from his army group to East Prussia. Several other divisions had been deactivated to provide additional personnel for the planned increase in armored divisions. But von Bock seems at first either to have miscalculated or disregarded the true purpose of all this activity. He seems not to have surmised that by

September 1940 Hitler had abandoned plans to invade England, that Hitler had already made the momentous decision to invade the Soviet Union not later than the spring of 1941, and that Hitler had ordered the Wehrmacht to prepare in strictest secrecy operational plans for that formidable undertaking.[2] Loath to involve himself in politics and grand strategy, Bock focused his attention for the time being on the air attacks over England. He was more inclined to leave to the higher authorities the problem of bringing the war to a successful conclusion, and he seemed to believe sincerely that England would soon be forced to conclude peace.[3]

Still he was not exactly displeased with the amassing of forces in the East. He remembered how the Russians had disrupted Germany's war plans in 1914, twenty-six years past, when Russian armies, driving with unexpected swiftness into East Prussia, had compelled the Imperial German High Command to divert troops from France just when the capture of Paris appeared to be imminent. This time, Field Marshal von Bock reflected, not only Paris but all Western Europe was in German hands, and it was therefore "a sound move to use our great military strength as security against a possible Russian threat."[4]

Immediately following his arrival in Berlin, Bock attended a series of conferences at Army High Command. The conferences were called by Army Commander-in-Chief von Brauchitsch. Chief of the General Staff Halder, army group commanders, and their chiefs of staff were asked to attend. There was no discussion of invading the Soviet Union at these conferences. The discussions centered upon technical matters: the most suitable locations of high military headquarters—including Bock's—in the East, logistics and communications, the structure and capability of the newly organized motorized and armored divisions, schedules of war games, and similar topics.

During one of the conferences von Bock agreed to Halder's suggestion that Posen, an old Polish city about midway between Berlin and Warsaw, should be the location for Headquarters, Army Group B. Bock agreed to the suggestion and also consented not to proceed at once to Posen to assume command, although his staff officers were already there. Instead, von Bock somewhat naively agreed to remain temporarily in Berlin.[5]

Both von Bock and Halder have stated that improper communications between Berlin and Posen was the reason that Bock was asked to remain a few days longer in Berlin. On the surface this may have been a valid consideration, although the German Army was technically capable of establishing communications between two principal locations within a very short time.

The real purpose for Bock's continued stay in Berlin, however, went beyond the technical matter of laying communications between Berlin and Posen. At the highest levels of the German military hierarchy a move was afoot to force Bock out of active service.[6] Bock had not been satisfied with the relatively secondary role that his army group had played during the Western campaign. He had expressed his dissatisfaction by consistently and often very cynically criticizing military operations in the Low Countries and in France. On occasions during the Western campaign, he had so vehemently opposed certain decisions at Army High Command that his opposition could be classified as outright insubordination. The school of younger German generals, the proponents of the so-far successful blitzkrieg concept, regarded von Bock as somewhat old-fashioned and inflexible in his professional approach to this new concept. More than once in the past von Bock had been extremely skeptical of thrusting deeply into enemy territory with armored columns. He contended that this unduly exposed the attacker's flanks to the enemy and jeopardized the operation.

Bock preferred the more conservative doctrine of the mass attack on a broad front, of closer coordination between infantry and armor and between ground forces and air power. The Wehrmacht's recent successes in Poland and in the West, in which fast-moving tank columns had advanced deeply into enemy territory without regard to flank security, had not caused von Bock to revise his conservative doctrinal approach appreciably.

Most of all, von Bock's cold, overbearing personality had incurred the wrath and even hatred of quite a few officers in the German Army. "It is extremely difficult to convince Bock," was a comment often heard both at Armed Forces High Command and at Army High Command. "Bock is a difficult man to serve," was a statement often made by his subordinate commanders.[7]

The question of von Bock's retention in the active service as army group commander was discussed in utmost secrecy at the highest military levels. By September 1940, it centered not upon retaining Bock—by then too many officers wanted to see him removed—but upon who would replace him. Here there was considerable disagreement. To resolve this thorny matter, Army High Command compiled a confidential list of officers who were considered, in descending order, Bock's most competent and acceptable replacement. Heading the list was Field Marshal Günther von Kluge, commander of the Fourth Army in Bock's Army Group B. Next were Field Marshals List and Walther von Reichenau. Reichenau was one of the relatively few professional officers who, along with Bock, had remained in active service during the prewar crises between Hitler and the Officers Corps. His qualifications were not rated as highly as List's or Kluge's, but he had embraced National Socialism with far more enthusiasm than most of his colleagues, and for this reason the anti-Bock officers thought he might find favor with Hitler. Two or three lower ranking officers, including a major general, completed the list.[8]

The controversy reached climactic proportions in mid-September, assuming a "now or never" peak. If Bock was to be removed from command, the time to do it was while he was in Berlin. Once he had assumed a field command again, it would be more difficult to dislodge him. The list of possible replacements was laid before Hitler on 14 or 15 September. On 17 September, Hitler arrived at a decision concerning Bock. He dismissed each name on the list with a curt remark and let it be known that he intended without equivocation to retain von Bock in active command.[9]

The factors that led Adolf Hitler to decide in favor of Bock are open to speculation. In his unfathomable, often unpredictable way, Hitler apparently saw in von Bock a professional officer who would not question Germany's political moves but would simply carry out military instructions. Hitler may have also regarded the Bock controversy as an opportunity to strengthen even more his authority over the Officers Corps and to show once again, as he had done two and a half years earlier during the Blomberg-Fritsch crisis, that he alone possessed the power to arbitrate controversies in the military hierarchy.

And so, Bock kept his command in September 1940. Publicly he disregarded the whole episode, if indeed he was aware of its intensity. On 21 September he prepared to leave Berlin for Posen but on the following day became seriously ill with stomach ulcers. He had long suffered from an ulcerated stomach; whether this condition was aggravated by the anti-Bock conspiracy, which Hitler had finally settled a few days before, is unclear. "My old stomach trouble is bothering me again," Bock wrote laconically, "but for the time being I shall exercise command of my army group from my sickbed!"[10]

He did not, as it turned out. Bock was to remain ill for four months. On 26 September, Army High Command, acting upon direct instructions from Hitler, granted Bock sick leave until 1 December. When that date arrived Bock was still physically unable to return to active duty, and his sick leave was extended indefinitely. From 26 September to 15 December his temporary replacement at Army Group B was Field Marshal List. On the latter date List was ordered to the Balkans and von Kluge, with Hitler's concurrence, became "acting" commander.

During Bock's long illness his detractors at higher headquarters apparently made no more attempts to displace him. As he lay abed his high colleagues called periodically and solicitously about his health. Field Marshal Wilhelm Keitel, Chief of Staff, Armed Forces High Command, visited him once or twice during his confinement. So did Brauchitsch, Halder, and several other officers from Army High Command. A particularly frequent caller was Bock's Chief of Staff, Lieutenant General Hans von Salmuth. Salmuth made the 250-mile trip between Posen and Berlin at least once a week to inform Bock of developments in the army group.

On 11 November 1940, the twenty-second anniversary of Germany's surrender in the First World War, Adolf Hitler came to see Bock. "The Führer sat at my bedside for a half hour. He was cordial and quite concerned about my health. . . . We discussed general matters. . . . Upon his departure the Führer wished me a speedy recovery."[11]

But von Bock's condition did not improve speedily. This depressed him, though he maintained an interest not only in affairs concerning his army group but in current developments. For the latter he relied chiefly on newspapers and radio broadcasts. At this time Bock did not have access to confidential military information, other than what he received from von Salmuth concerning his own command.

On 3 December, von Bock's sixtieth birthday, Hitler again called.

The Führer brought a small gift and offered birthday congratulations. . . . After some preliminary inquiries about my health, he told me that it will be necessary to eradicate the Soviet Union from the face of the earth. Then England will rapidly lose her remaining influence in the world. I was somewhat surprised by the Führer's statement and remarked that Russia's enormous terrain and untested military strength would make this a difficult task, even for our powerful forces. The Führer's manner became cold and stiff, and he replied rather sharply that it was Germany's destiny to launch this great crusade against Bolshevism. . . . Before he left, however, the Führer was once more friendly and expressed the hope that I would soon be well, for he expected me to play a decisive role in the forthcoming crusade against Soviet Russia. . . .[12]

In this manner von Bock learned for the first time that Germany was preparing for war against Soviet Russia. It is ironical that he learned this not through normal military channels but from Hitler himself.

During the following weeks, Bock's condition gradually improved. On 18 December, List called to exchange farewells before his departure for the Balkans and to thank Bock for the privilege of having commanded Army Group B. On the same day Halder telephoned that pending Bock's final recovery, von Kluge would represent von Bock at conferences called by Army High Command.

Also on that same day in the Reich Chancellory, Hitler affixed his signature to a lengthy, top-secret document entitled Directive No. 21, Operation *Barbarossa*. The document dictated that "the Wehrmacht must be prepared *to destroy Soviet Russia in a blitzkrieg campaign, even before the end of the war with England.* . . . [and that] the exact date for the start of the campaign will be issued eight weeks in advance. . . ."[13]

Bock did not see the document immediately. He spent the holiday season of 1940 in quiet recuperation. On Christmas Eve, Hitler addressed the elite *SS-Leibstandarte "Adolf Hitler"* in Berlin's Sportspalast. The address was broadcast to the German nation. Hitler used the occasion to proclaim that Germany now stood at the peak of her power, that her enemies—especially England—were foolish to continue resistance, and that the following year would be decisive in the conduct of the war. Bock listened in his apartment, remembered Hitler's words a few weeks before, and waited for his physical condition to improve sufficiently, so he could take an active part in the forthcoming "decisive year of the war."

On 2 January 1941 von Salmuth and several staff aides arrived in Berlin and went straight to Bock's apartment. Salmuth brought along a copy of Directive No. 21 and a supplementary top-secret order from Army High Command, which instructed Army Group B to prepare an operational study "in the event of war with Soviet Russia."[14] As Bock studied the documents some of his old bitterness toward Army High Command returned. "It is incredible that I must learn about these things from my subordinates!"[15] Nevertheless, Bock warmed to the task and agreed with Salmuth that military operations against Soviet Russia must first of all take into account the vastness and relative technical backwardness of the country, and that it would be absolutely necessary to destroy Russia's military forces along the western border before they could retreat eastward across the Duna-Dnieper rivers.

After conferring with Bock, Salmuth hurried back to Posen, and in two weeks he submitted the study to Army High Command. In essence, the study reflected the same operational concepts that had been set forth in Directive No. 21. It also expressed the same optimism—an optimism that "can be explained only in the light of the Wehrmacht's easy victories in Poland and France."[16] The study concurred in the Wehrmacht's plan to employ three army groups on a broad front in Soviet Russia. It agreed that the central army group—Bock's—should be the strongest, should bear the brunt of the assault, and should advance rapidly north of the Pripet Marshes in the direction of Smolensk, destroying in the process enemy forces in White Russia. But in contrast to Directive No. 21, the study proposed that Leningrad and Kronstadt be bypassed and that the bulk of the Wehrmacht's strength—with Bock commanding—should be concentrated in the central army group area, to exploit the destruction of Russian forces and to capture Moscow as quickly as possible. This proposal was rejected at Army High Command.[17] Leningrad, Kronstadt, and Kiev, as well as Moscow, remained terrain objectives to be attained in conjunction with the major aim of destroying Russia's armed power.

The reason for Bock's proposal to bypass Leningrad and Kronstadt is clear. Since the responsibility for executing the major effort in the attack fell upon him, Bock was reluctant to see forces diverted to what he considered to be secondary objectives. He did not want to run the risk of weakening the German forces by diffusing their strength all over Western Russia. To Bock, the capture of the Soviet Russian capital and main communications center was of greatest importance, second only to the rapid destruction of the Russian military forces. The fact that his army group was to be assigned this task enhanced his pride and revitalized his determination. In the capture of Moscow, Bock foresaw the honor that would accrue to him, the fame that would be his for achieving the feat that had spelled disaster to warriors of past history, to Charles XII and Napoleon Bonaparte. He foresaw in the capture of Moscow the crowning achievement of a long and honorable military career, a career in which he had subordinated every aspect of his life to the glory of the Fatherland, except his own personal ambitions.

And Bock also foresaw, quite practically, that imposing upon the Wehrmacht the formidable task of capturing simultaneously widespread terrain objectives reduced the chances of attaining any single objective. It is of more than passing interest that Field Marshal von Bock, who was now consumed with the idea of being the first modern conqueror of Moscow, set aside his conservative approach to Germany's new doctrine of warfare. No longer was he concerned with exposing his flanks to the enemy. No longer was he obsessed with the idea of infantry and armor keeping pace with each other, or more explicitly, with armor adjusting its pace to the advancing infantry. Bock was prepared to subordinate all considerations to the destruction of Russian military forces and the conquest of Moscow.

On 31 January 1941, for the first time in over four months, von Bock reported for active duty. He was not sure if and when his stomach trouble would recur but he felt well enough to face the crucial days that lay ahead. His first business was to attend a conference at Brauchitsch's headquarters for army group and army commanders. Bock arrived early at the conference, looking even leaner than in the past, but rested and fit.

When the conference began, Bock quickly discerned that a pessimistic attitude prevailed.

Brauchitsch paints a bleak picture. . . . The attack against England has been definitely cancelled; Germany's plan to involve Spain in the war has failed; and the Italians are in a bad way in North Africa. . . . Brauchitsch discussed in detail the forthcoming operations against Russia and stressed the importance of annihilating Russian forces in the border zones so that German forces could rapidly gain freedom of movement. I asked Halder, sitting next to me: "What assurance do we have that the Russians will sit still in front of the Duna-Dnieper while we destroy them?" Halder smiled wanely and merely reiterated Brauchitsch's words.[18]

On the next day, as Bock was preparing to leave at last for Posen, he received a call from Hitler's personal adjutant, Colonel Rudolf Schmundt, asking him to report to Hitler. The session with Hitler lasted almost an hour.

The Führer was cordial and expressed pleasure that I was again well. . . . In contrast to the pessimism at Army High Command yesterday, he regards Russia's collapse as a foregone conclusion. . . . I remarked that we can defeat the Russians if they stand and fight, but it may be difficult to convince them to talk in terms of peace. The Führer replied that we are militarily and economically in excellent condition and if the Russians continue to resist after the Ukraine and Moscow have been conquered we will simply advance all the way to Siberia. . . . "Nevertheless," I told him, "we should be prepared for reverses." Hitler replied pointedly: "I am convinced that they will think a hurricane has hit them!" As in past meetings with the Führer I noticed that his attitude changed quickly from warm friendliness to cold suspicion and back again. . . . We parted cordially and he wished me well in Posen.[19]

Bock left Berlin early on the morning of 3 February. At the Posen railroad station he found that a grand reception had been prepared for his arrival. In the reception were Gauleiter (district commissioner) Arthur Greiser of Wartheland (of which Posen was the capital), as well as Posen's mayor, some lesser civil officials, and all the generals, about two hundred, who were assigned to Bock's Army Group Center. A large honor guard and a military band were present. The band played Bock's favorite march, "Preussens Gloria." Gauleiter Greiser; Field Marshal von Kluge; Colonel Generals Adolf Strauss, Heinz Guderian, and Hermann Hoth; and a few other high officers made short speeches of welcome. Von Bock was flattered, though in the circumstances he would have preferred a less flamboyant reception. But he thanked everyone and used the opportunity to exhort his listeners to greater efforts during the glorious but difficult days to come.[20]

In Posen, Bock settled down to the task of reacquainting himself with his command. For the first few days he spent long hours at his desk, studying piles of reports. He conferred with his subordinate commanders and staff officers, approved map exercises and war games that were scheduled from army group to corps and divisions in preparation for the forthcoming attack, and busied himself with numerous personnel and technical matters related to command of a vast military organization comprising over a million men.

Among the constant stream of callers at Bock's headquarters during the days following his arrival was a young officer from Army High Command who identified himself as Colonel Horst Rathke. Under the pretext of discussing confidential personnel affairs with von Bock, Rathke requested a private audience, which Bock granted. After some preliminaries, Rathke stated that he represented a group of officers at Army High Command who were convinced that Germany should not undertake military operations against Soviet Russia while England was still a belligerent and that a number of senior officers at Army High Command were conspiring most secretly to stage a *coup d'état* in Berlin to save Germany from doom. Rathke asked von Bock to associate himself with the conspiracy. At this, Field Marshal von Bock exploded in anger and summarily dismissed Rathke with the statement that it was utter nonsense even to consider such a thing.[21] So far as is known, Bock was not approached again by any member of an anti-Hitler conspiracy until very late in the war.

Throughout February and early March, Bock busied himself with supervising preparations for the forthcoming attack. He made an attempt to visit most of the more than fifty divisions under his command at least once during the period. He conferred with army, corps, and division commanders; inspected regiments and battalions; and talked to privates, corporals, and sergeants. He found to his great pleasure that morale was generally excellent, though a few soldiers in some units dared to inform their field marshal that there was a shortage of rations. Bock instructed his chief supply officer, Major General Ludwig Kübler, to determine what remedial measure could be taken and was informed, to his displeasure, that Army High Command had scheduled even a further curtailment of the daily rations. "I am not so sure about all this," Bock noted. "If the rations are being reduced now, what will happen when we have moved into Russia's interior, far from our bases of supply?"[22] Once more, as during the recent Western campaign, Bock began to complain to Army High Command about this and other matters, but he was unsuccessful in preventing a reduction of food rations and other vital supplies in his army group.

During the numerous war games and map exercises that took place, Bock often arbitrated disputes between his strong-willed senior commanders and found it necessary to assert his authority as army group commander. On one occasion, his Ninth Army commander, Strauss, and his Panzer Group 3 commander, Hoth, engaged in a heated discussion during a conference at Bock's headquarters regarding the coordination of infantry and armor. Hoth vigorously opposed the assignment of infantry divisions to his panzer group in the forthcoming attack. He contended that this would hinder his advance. Strauss took an opposite viewpoint, stating that the basic principle of command unity was being violated if Hoth would command only armored troops but not supporting infantry.

Bock overrode Hoth in this case and ordered five infantry divisions, about 70,000 men, to be assigned to Hoth's Panzer Group 3. Bock explained to both Hoth and Strauss that Russia's limited, inferior road network would become quickly congested and that Hoth, the commander of armor in the projected Ninth Army Area, must exercise authority over both the advancing tanks and infantry. Then Hoth could order infantry off the roads if there developed a danger of hindering tanks. On another occasion, Bock settled a similar dispute between von Kluge, commander of the Fourth Army, and Guderian, commander of Panzer Group 2.[23]

In contests such as these, Bock seemed reluctant to aggrieve his senior commanders, though this would later prove to be unavoidable. He was apparently sincere in his desire for harmony within his enormous, complex command. Perhaps the events of September 1940 had taught Bock a lesson. But most of all, he realized as an experienced professional soldier that he could never accomplish the preponderous task that had been placed before him without the loyalty, cooperation, and coordination of his senior officers, the men who would make the on-the-spot estimates and decisions in the field.

Despite his good intentions, however, the only senior officer with whom Bock maintained consistently good relations throughout the preparatory stages for the assault on Russia, and even during the hectic, confused days following the assault, was his air fleet commander, Field Marshal Albert Kesselring.[24]

During the months of preparation preceding the attack, Bock determined not to overlook any factor that might tend to detract from his chances of success. Among the many developments to which he paid particular attention were the intelligence reports compiled at the army, corps, and divisional commands and submitted to his headquarters. One such report is indicative of von Bock's attitude toward the forthcoming attack. On 11 March Major General Hans von Obernitz, who commanded Bock's 293rd Infantry Division, delivered personally to Bock an intelligence report that stated that the Russians were carrying out extensive training maneuvers in the area south of Vilna, Lithuania. Obernitz was excited about the report, for the agent who had furnished it claimed that the Russian maneuvers were but a camouflage for a planned attack on Germany. Bock calmed Obernitz and tended to disregard the report. At the same time, however, he reflected that it was impossible to conceal the huge concentration of German troops along the German-Russian demarcation line in Poland, that the Russians certainly knew something was afoot and were probably taking countermeasures.[25]

On 12 March von Salmuth signed, by command of von Bock, the fateful operations order for the attack. The operations order, classified top secret, was given very limited distribution—one to each of Bock's three armies, one to each panzer group, and information copies to Army Commander-in-Chief Brauchitsch and Chief of the General Staff Halder. As directed by Army High Command's order of 31 January, Army Group B set 15 May 1941 as the date for the attack on Soviet Russia. The operations order stated in surprisingly simple military terminology the army group's mission:

The army group will attack in a northeasterly direction and, supported by strong flanking forces, will destroy the enemy in White Russia. Panzer Group 3 will attack with its motorized and armored units north of Minsk; it will be followed by Fourth Army. Once Minsk is bypassed these forces will join together in the vicinity of Borrisov-Orsha, in order to advance rapidly towards Smolensk. Upon conquest of Smolensk all forces, including the reserve Second Army, will join with the northern, or left-flank, army group for a *rapid advance* to Moscow.[26]

The operations order estimated the enemy's strength confronting the army group at about fifty divisions, or about 800,000 men. About two-thirds of this force was concentrated around Bialystok in Poland; the remaining one-third was located near Minsk. The entire force was called the West Front and was commanded by Colonel General D. P. Pavlov. The operations order gave no estimate when Smolensk would be reached. Its estimate of Russian military strength was quite accurate, and its general tone was that the Russians, although approximately equal in numerical strength, were inferior in quality and must be surprised and overwhelmed in the shortest possible time.

On the same day that Bock's army group distributed the operations order for the attack, Bock noted in his diary that the United States had passed the Lend-Lease Act. He was despondent and stated that ". . . . They (the United States) have done everything now except actually send troops to Europe. . . ."[27]

During these weeks Bock made several trips from Posen to Berlin on official business. The trips afforded little time for the relaxation that Bock felt he needed occasionally for health reasons. On 18 March, however, he relaxed by attending the formal re-opening, under German auspices, of the opera theater in Posen. Several high officials, including Propaganda Minister Dr. Josef Goebbels, came from Berlin for the event. During the intermission Bock spoke briefly with Goebbels. Preparations for the attack were, under the circumstances, progressing smoothly, Bock told Goebbels. The latter, in turn, told Bock that there were many inherent difficulties in Germany's propaganda effort and that he, Goebbels, was having a hard time convincing the phlegmatic, stubborn English that their cause was hopeless. "Goebbels seemed preoccupied," Bock noted, "and he is not overly enthusiastic about the attack."[28]

The last week of March and early April was an eventful

time for Field Marshal von Bock. On 27 March he journeyed to Berlin to attend a conference at Army High Command. He was gloomy and dissatisfied with the results of the conference. Brauchitsch told Bock that it was imperative for the armored groups to make contact immediately east of Minsk. Bock protested that this was too restrictive and that not only would the swampy terrain along the Beresina River endanger a link-up of his armored forces in the area, but it was of greatest importance that those forces advance rapidly, without regard to conjoining with each other, until they reached Smolensk.

They (Army High Command) concern themselves with small details and refuse to comprehend the ramifications and implications of the operation from an overall standpoint! I am unable to get clear answers to my questions. What happens, for instance, if the Russians counterattack before we reach Minsk? Is it incumbent on my authority to decide when and where to cross the Dnieper? I insist that it should be, but they evade the issue.[29]

Bock remained in Berlin for several days. On the day after the conference, 28 March, he attended a breakfast at the Reich Chancellory honoring the Japanese Foreign Minister, Yosuke Matsuoka. Bock sat between Brauchitsch and the Japanese Ambassador to Berlin, General Hiroshi Oshima. The occasion was a pleasant one for Bock and seemed to assuage his frustrations of the day before. He noted that General Oshima was an extremely intellectual person and was in accord with Germany's great calling to destroy Russian Communism.

On 30 March Bock again went to the Reich Chancellory to hear Hitler deliver an address to all of the high officers of the Wehrmacht. Hitler spoke for four hours. After reviewing the world situation, he reiterated the necessity for destroying Soviet Russia and the major objectives of the forthcoming attack. All of this was in order, as far as Bock was concerned. But then Hitler told his listeners that the war against Soviet Russia must be a different kind of war, a war of ideological, racial, and political opposites.

The war will be such that it cannot be conducted in knightly fashion. ... It must be waged with unprecedented, merciless, and unrelenting harshness. All officers must rid themselves of old-fashioned and obsolete theories. I know that the necessity for making war in such a manner is beyond the comprehension of you generals, but I cannot and will not change my orders and I insist that they be carried out with unquestioning and unconditional obedience.[30]

Bock did not like this at all. As Hitler spoke, he turned in astonishment first to Brauchitsch, then to Halder, and asked: "What does the Führer mean? Will we have to shoot civilians and noncombatants?"[31] Bock claimed that again he received evasive replies, but it would not be the last time he would protest with great vigor the conduct of the war in Soviet Russia.

That same evening Hitler held a reception for the Army High Command and the generals commanding in the East. Hitler was a congenial host and moved freely and easily among his guests. As in past meetings he was cordial with Bock and inquired about his health. Hitler then stressed upon Bock the importance of giving free rein to his armored forces after the breakout beyond Minsk and of coordinating with the northern forces the capture of both Leningrad and Moscow. In his outspoken manner Bock stated to the Führer that this might be a difficult proposition and therefore the greater effort should be made to capture Moscow. If nothing else, Bock stated, this would simplify the army's tasks, for the control of the armored forces in carrying out a dual mission might become very complex. Further, Bock told the Führer, he was not so certain about the general policy for the conduct of the war. The Russians, he was convinced, should be regarded as combatants according to the international rules of warfare, or else "we may find them to be a rather tenacious enemy."[32]

Hitler's reaction to Bock's comments are not known, though it may be assumed that Hitler was less than pleased with Bock's remarks. Bock noted later that at the precise moment when Hitler was about to retort, von Brauchitsch appeared at Hitler's side and "chimed in" with a few comments of his own, designed to indicate his support of Hitler's general policies. Brauchitsch, according to Bock, made reference to the necessity for maintaining close liaison between the forces in the East and that, further, the laws of international warfare were subject to change as conditions dictated. The result was that for Bock the matter remained unclarified.[33]

On 1 April Army High Command issued an order defining the organization and subordination of forces in the East. Von Bock's Army Group B was redesignated Army Group Center. On Bock's left flank was Field Marshal Wilhelm Ritter von Leeb's army group. It was renamed Army Group North. On his right Field Marshal von Rundstedt's forces became Army Group South.

Army Group Center was the strongest of the three. Officially it comprised three infantry armies—the Second, Fourth and Ninth—and two armored groups, which had the equivalent strength of armies. The order stated that until Army Group Center's breakthrough at Smolensk had been achieved, the Second Army, commanded by Colonel General Maximilian Freiherr von Weichs, would remain in army reserve. Thus Bock's enormous command, including Second Army, comprised one cavalry, seven motorized, eleven armored, and fifty-three infantry divisions and an air fleet for a total of about 1,200,000 soldiers and airmen. Army Group Center was the largest military force, under the command of one officer, ever assembled in the annals of military history.

On 6 April the Balkan campaign began. The German forces, commanded by Bock's colleague, List, attacked Yugoslavia and Greece with such fury that those two nations were overrun within days. Army High Command moved its headquarters to Pressburg on the Danube River, to conduct the operations from a closer vantage point. On the same day the Armed Forces High Command postponed the attack on Soviet Russia for thirty days, or until 15 June 1941.

In his headquarters at Posen, Bock went ahead with preparations for the attack. He experienced during the following weeks a curious mixture of both concern and relief. He was concerned lest the postponement of the attack would result in a lowering of troop morale and efficiency as had happened in the Polish and Western campaigns. He was relieved that he might possibly have time, due to the postponement, to resolve differences in policy regarding the conduct of the war between himself and Army High Command.

During the second week of April he conducted still another map exercise, which involved his army, armored group, and corps commanders. As a result of the exercise, Bock decided that the southern armored force, Guderian's Panzer Group 2, should carry the main weight of the initial assault. He was still concerned, however, about the left flank of Guderian's armored forces because of the danger that the tanks and auxiliary vehicles, by closely skirting the Pripet Marshes in their advance, would become bogged down. Guderian contemptuously dismissed this danger, and Bock relented, though reserving the right to alter the direction of the advance if conditions required.

Early in May, Bock's senior staff officer, von Salmuth, was transferred to Army Group North to take command of XXX Infantry Corps. "Salmuth long has been my trusted colleague in peace and in war," Bock commented. "I prefer not to lose him, but I am glad that he is finally receiving an assignment as a commander. He has been a staff officer for a long time. . . ."[34] Salmuth's transfer caused yet another altercation between Bock and Halder. Since information about Salmuth's successor was not immediately forthcoming from Army High Command, Bock called up Halder to inquire about Salmuth's replacement. Halder suggested Major General Anton von Greiffenberg, who had recently taken part in the Balkan campaign and was now on leave. Bock did not know Greiffenberg personally and notified Halder that he wanted to think about the matter for a day or two. Without waiting for Bock's response, Halder, according to Bock, appointed Greiffenberg to be chief of staff, Army Group Center. Bock was furious that Halder would act upon an important matter without his concurrence and wasted no time in so informing Halder. "And besides, I lose, unfortunately, two other general staff officers at the same time, the competent Gröben and my staff intelligence officer, Colonel Manthey. Both are interested in acquiring command assignments, and though I am reluctant, I consent to release them from my headquarters."[35]

During the remainder of May and early June, von Bock traveled considerably either between Posen and Berlin or on inspection tours to his widely scattered units. For four days in mid-May he journeyed by special train along the German-Russian demarcation line in Fourth Army's area, accompanied by Field Marshal von Kluge. On the second day of the trip Brauchitsch telegraphed that he intended to visit Army Group Center at Posen. Instead of returning to Posen to meet Brauchitsch, Bock rather strangely decided to adhere to his inspection schedule and delegated Kluge to represent him at Posen. Bock visited and conferred with most of the corps and a few division commanders in Fourth Army, and again he manifested an interest in talking to individual soldiers of all ranks. "Everywhere the troops give a happy, fresh impression," Bock noted, "but when I ask if there are sufficient supplies they answer: 'Yes sir, but we could use more!' And on 1 June the meat ration will again be reduced! I wonder if they (Army High Command) intend to fight this war with guns alone!"[36]

Returning from the inspection tour, Bock arranged to meet Kluge in Warsaw. He made suggestions to Kluge to improve conditions in Fourth Army, and then he learned that Kluge was unhappy about his conference with Brauchitsch. Brauchitsch wanted to change Fourth Army's operational plans. Kluge contested this on the basis that too little time remained. Bock agreed with Kluge, in this case, and assured him the plans would not be changed.

This is a curious episode. Why did not Bock himself elect to confer with Brauchitsch, his immediate superior? A probable answer is that relations between the officers had been very strained since Hitler's reception at the Reich Chancellory in late March, and Bock, perhaps to assert his own independence, chose not to confer with Brauchitsch at that particular time. Adding to the irony of the entire scope of relationships between the men in whose hands the fate of Germany rested is that shortly thereafter Bock and Kluge became estranged. A day or two after their Warsaw meeting, Kluge, apparently upon reflection, wrote a personal letter to Bock. In the letter Kluge complained that his authority was being impinged upon and demanded more freedom in the exercise of his command, or else he wished to be relieved. Bock replied with a sharply worded letter, pointing out again the deficiencies he had found in Kluge's Fourth Army during his recent inspection tour, informing Kluge that "responsibility for command of the army group is *mine* and, consequently, I shall not permit myself to be inhibited by your demands."[37]

Although Bock's letter to Kluge seemed to have settled

the immediate issue, it did not dispel, but rather increased, animosity between the two officers.

Late in May, Bock went on a similar inspection tour to the Ninth Army, the bulk of whose troops were concentrated in the Suwalki area. Again Bock found troop morale to be relatively high, though in his perfectionist manner he noted deficiencies in Strauss' army. He also noted that the landscape around Suwalki was desolate and the populace was rather provincial, if not primitive, and appeared to be "afraid and suspicious."[38]

Upon his return to Posen a secret directive was awaiting him. The document announced that the attack on Soviet Russia was postponed until 22 June 1941. On 4 June he received still another startling directive from Army High Command. This directive had been written in consequence of Hitler's secret verbal instructions to the German Armed Forces during the Berlin conference in March. It stated that political commissars attached to the Soviet Russian armies were not to be treated as prisoners of war but were to be summarily executed upon capture. The directive further stated that every German soldier had the right to shoot any Russian soldier or civilian whom he suspected of guerrilla activity, regardless of the circumstances. The directive conceded that its intent breached international law. To circumvent this, Hitler formally absolved the German soldier, from that point forward, of all guilt for his actions in the forthcoming campaign, "provided that the breaking of a civil law, such as murder, rape, or robbery, was not involved."[39]

Von Bock was outraged. Immediately, he attempted to contact von Brauchitsch by telephone to inform him that the order was intolerable, that it violated rudimentary principles of modern warfare, and that it would destroy military discipline in his command and therefore could not and would not be executed. Bock failed to reach Brauchitsch by telephone. He then called Halder and told him substantially the same thing that he had intended to tell Brauchitsch. Halder replied that he would inform Brauchitsch but could not promise that the order would be appreciably modified. Halder agreed that in effect the directive disregarded generally accepted military standards and procedure but advised Bock that there was little he could do about it.

By 7 June no response to Bock's furious telephone calls had been received at Army Group Center. So he telephoned Brauchitsch again. This time he persuaded Brauchitsch to discuss the matter and again stated in positive terms that he did not subscribe to the indiscriminate shooting of Russian civilians and political commissars. Brauchitsch demurred but promised to call back. Within the hour he did and told Bock that the "spirit" of the directive remained the same, that the German high law courts had ruled on the contents of the directive, that it was legal to protect or avenge oneself from partisan or guerrilla attack of any kind, and that the basic laws of warfare were not affected. After a prolonged debate, Bock adopted a "so-this-is-the-way-you-want-it" attitude and concluded the conversation. Privately, he resolved to modify the order and to conduct military courts for the administration and dispensation of justice in Russia so long as this did not constitute an unduly heavy administrative workload in his command.

On 12 June, Guderian came to see von Bock with a new proposal for the integration of armored and infantry units. Bock rejected the proposal on the basis that he saw nothing new or advantageous in it. Later he confided cynically to his diary that Guderian did not have the personality to command fifteen divisions. "I suppose everyone is guilty at times of not knowing exactly what one wants!"[40]

Two days later Bock was again called to Berlin for conference with Hitler. In his last address to his assembled generals before the attack began, Hitler repeated the reasons for and the objective of the campaign. Bock did not discern anything new in the speech. On this trip he remained aloof and noncommittal regarding the controversial political commissar order from Hitler, having already decided that he would, as far as he and the officers and men of Army Group Center were concerned, disregard it.

Bock spent the last few days before Attack Day at his headquarters at Posen. On the afternoon of 20 June, von Brauchitsch issued a coded message stating the approximate time of the attack and instructed Army Group Center to coordinate the exact minute with Army Group North and South. Bock was thunderstruck. "Suddenly at the last moment we lose coordination," he lamented, "all because Brauchitsch himself does not have the courage or ability to pinpoint the exact time! I check with Rundstedt, with whom I have good liaison; he agrees that 3:10 A. M. is all right. But Leeb wants to attack ten minutes sooner! We all three finally agree on 3:15 A. M. Once again it is I who must suffer because of Brauchitsch's irresoluteness!"[41]

On the eve of the great assault, Bock read stacks of intelligence reports and later received in his offices a "certain civil official" who had just arrived from Moscow. The official pleaded with Bock to use his influence as a high military leader to stop the war. The official informed Bock that while the Russians expected war they had no idea when it would come and were sincerely trying to abide by their commitments to Germany according to the Non-Aggression Pact of 1939. Bock was condescending and sympathetic. But he assured his caller that even if all the colossal preparations and plans had not been made it was still too late to prevent the war and that any action by him in that direction at that last moment could be termed only as mutiny. Moreover, Bock assured his listener that it was Germany's magnanimous destiny to erase the scourge of communism from the world and to bring cultural and political freedom to the Russian peoples. No other time in modern history, Bock stated, was probably more appropriate to carry out this grand mission than now, and at no time would Germany be better prepared.[42]

Later on during that last evening of peace between Germany and Russia in 1941, Bock also received a call from his colleague, Field Marshal Kesselring, commander of Air Fleet 2, Army Group Center. "Kesselring is friendly, relaxed, and ever ready to cooperate, as usual," Bock noted. "Still the two of us feel heavily weighed down with the awesome responsibilities that now confront us."[43]

After instructing an orderly to awaken him at 2:30 A. M., Bock retired early.

Exactly at 3:15 A. M., 22 June 1941, German artillery opened a concentrated, devastating fire all along Soviet Russia's western border, from the Baltic to the Black Sea. Five minutes later, as dawn broke serenely in the east, German aircraft droned in swarms across the demarcation line, on their way to bombard predesignated targets—airdromes, troop concentrations, and supply depots—in Soviet Russia. On the ground, Germany's East Army, a vast war machine of three and a half million highly trained men, with thousands of tanks, trucks, armored cars, and vehicles of all descriptions, with tons of equipment and supplies, began to assail Soviet Russia. The greatest land war in history had begun.

At about the same moment, Bock sat down at his desk, a cup of diluted coffee in his hand, to await first reports from his troops in the gigantic contest.

1. Tippelskirch, pp. 198–200. The most common pretext was participation in training maneuvers on the flatlands of East Prussia and Poland.

2. Hitler's decision to attack Soviet Russia evolved during the summer of 1940. The exact date, if there was one, is not known. In early July 1940 Colonel General Alfred Jodl, Chief of Operations, Armed Forces High Command, one of Hitler's closest confidants, disclosed to a small, select group of officers that military operations against Soviet Russia were contemplated in early 1941. See Tippelskirch, p. 199. In late August 1940 the German Armed Forces High Command distributed on a limited basis a top-secret, carefully worded document entitled *Operation Aufbau Ost,* Operation Eastern Construction. The document did not mention Soviet Russia, but its implication was significant. See Wheeler-Bennett, pp. 509–10.

3. Von Bock KTB, 1 September 1940. On that date Bock recorded in his diary that the English doubtlessly could not sustain the German air attacks beyond the beginning of autumn.

4. *Ibid.,* 8 September 1940.

5. Halder KTB, II, 10 September 1940, p. 94. There is some conflict in dates between Halder's and Bock's diaries. Bock states that he arrived in Berlin on 11 September and that this particular conference took place on 13 September. See von Bock KTB, 13 September 1940.

6. The entire episode regarding Bock's retention or nonretention in the active military service in 1940 is strangely obfuscated. So far as is known, there is one veiled published reference to the episode. This is in Halder's war diary, in which he states matter of factly that Hitler had rejected a suggestion to replace Bock with Major General Erich Marcks, who was then Chief of Staff of the Eighteenth Army. See Halder KTB, II, 17 September 1940, p. 103.

7. B. H. Liddell Hart, *The German Generals Talk* (New York, 1948), p. 181. Several former Wehrmacht officers with whom the writer came into official contact during post-WWII years corroborated the fact that Bock was incorrigibly stubborn and often unreasonable in his relations with subordinate officers in his command. (Personal interviews with Major Generals Anton Freiherr von Bechtolsheim and Anton Grasser and with Brigadier General Oskar Munzel, 1953 and 1956.)

8. The major general was Erich Marcks. See n. 6.

9. The officer who related this information to the writer is a former member of Hitler's personal military staff and, when last contacted in

1962, was a member of the West German Federal Border Police. He asked that his name be held in confidence.

10. Von Bock KTB, 22 September 1940.

11. *Ibid.*, 11 November 1940.   12. 3 December 1940.

13. There are numerous published accounts of Directive No. 21, Operation *Barbarossa*. See H. R. Trevor-Roper, *Hitler's War Directives: 1939-1945* (London, 1964), p. 48; Walter Hubatsch, *Hitlers Weisungen für die Kriegsführung* (Stuttgart, 1959), p. 84; Guderian, p. 455; and others. The italics are Hitler's.

14. Von Bock KTB, 3 January 1941.   15. *Ibid.*

16. Tippelskirch, p. 202.

17. Von Bock KTB, 21 January 1941.

18. *Ibid.*, 31 January 1941.   19. 2 February 1941.

20. *Ibid.*, 3 February 1941. Bock mentions only that he was gratified with the reception and thanked those who had assembled. Colonel General Guderian, who was present at the reception, remembered some years later that Bock made an impassioned speech. (Personal interview with Colonel General Guderian, Germany, 1951.)

21. *Ibid.*, 7 February 1941. Wheeler-Bennett, in his comprehensive account of the anti-Hitler conspiracies prior to and during the Second World War, states that von Bock's headquarters were "indeed a nest of intrigue and treason." Wheeler-Bennett criticizes Bock for his failure to take an active part in the conspiracies. He states that Bock "was not the stuff of which the leaders of a military conspiracy are made. . . . Though he despised National Socialism and found repellent its increasing blood-lust, he was consumed with vanity and egotism, and the insignificance of his character prevented him from lifting a finger to overthrow a system for which he felt nothing but contempt. . . ." In contrast to Bock's own statement regarding the matter, Wheeler-Bennet contends that von Bock "was among the many whose response to the approaches of the conspirators was 'If it succeeds, I'll support you, but I won't take the consequences of failure!' " See Wheeler-Bennett, pp. 428ff. See also Fabian von Schlabrendorff, *Offiziere gegen Hitler* (Zurich, 1946), pp. 86–88.

22. Von Bock KTB, 17 February 1941.

23. *Ibid.*, 15 March—15 April 1941. Von Bock devotes many lines in his diary to his concern for harmony within Army Group Center during this period.

24. Bock liked and respected Field Marshal Kesselring, who was

known among his compatriots as "Smiling Al." Bock refers to him frequently as "my dear friend and comrade." *Ibid.*, 26 February 1941 *et passim*.

25. *Ibid.*, 11 March 1941.

26. *Heeresgruppe Mitte Kriegstagebuch*, microfilm no. 216/36091/647 U.S. National Archives (Washington, D.C.: 1966). Hereafter cited as H. Gp. Mitte KTB. The italics are from the original.

27. Von Bock KTB, 12 March 1941.   28. *Ibid.*, 18 March 1941.

29. *Ibid.*, 27 March 1941. The penchant of the Army High Command for minor details was a main reason for Bock's criticisms.

30. Wheeler-Bennett, p. 513.

31. Von Bock KTB, 31 March 1941.   32. *Ibid.*   33. *Ibid.*

34. *Ibid.*, 2 May 1941. Salmuth was promoted to Colonel General in 1943 and commanded the German Fifteenth Army in France until relieved because of illness in 1944. See Tippelskirch, p. 328.

35. *Ibid.*, von Bock does not further identify the officers.

36. *Ibid.*, 17 May 1941.

37. *Ibid.*, 21 May 1941. The italics are Bock's. He and Kluge were never on friendly terms after the episode of September 1940. Kluge was directly involved in the July 1944 plot to assassinate Hitler. He was commander of the Seventh Army during that period and shortly after committed suicide. He was buried without military honors. See Wheeler-Bennett, p. 674; Felix Gilbert, *Hitler Directs His War* (New York, 1950), p. 51; and Erich Zimmermann and Hans-Adolf Jacobsen (eds.), *Deutsche gegen Hitler* (Bonn, 1964), p. 21.

38. *Ibid.*, 27 May 1941.

39. Halder KTB, II, 3 June 1941, p. 434.

40. Von Bock KTB, 12 June 1941.   41. *Ibid.*, 20 June 1941.

42. Von Bock does not identify this "certain civil official," but it is safe to assume he was a member of the German Embassy in Moscow. The German Ambassador to Russia in 1941, Friedrich Werner Graf von der Schulenberg, was a bitter opponent of the war and was executed in November 1944 for his implication in the July 1944 anti-Hitler plot. See Wheeler-Bennett, p. 752, and Zimmermann and Jacobsen, p. 218. It is most probable that the official's visit to von Bock on the very eve of the attack represented a final, desperate attempt by von der Schulenberg to prevent the war.

43. Von Bock KTB, 21 June 1941.

WITHIN AN HOUR

after the massive assault began, teletype messages from Bock's forces far to the front were pouring into Headquarters, Army Group Center. The first reports had a confident, laudatory tone. Guderian's advance elements, comprising the XLVII Panzer Corps commanded by General der Panzertruppen Joachim Lemelsen, had crossed the Bug River and were already bypassing the fortress city of Brest-Litovsk. The Russians had apparently made no preparations to destroy the bridges; these had fallen intact into German hands.

Farther to the north, around Bialystok, Hoth's tanks had overrun the surprised Russians in their border outposts and were heading for Grodno on the Nieman River, some thirty miles eastward, to seize important river crossings. Still other reports that Bock read during those first tense moments indicated that motorized reconnaissance battalions from both the Fourth and Ninth Armies had crossed the Bug and Desna rivers at several places, were following closely behind the armored columns, and were meeting only sporadic Russian resistance.

At 7:00 A. M., 22 June, Bock boarded his private airplane. He was accompanied by his personal aides-de-camp, Colonel Heinrich Graf von Lehndorff and Major Hans Graf von Hardenberg (descendant of the great Prussian chancellor). About two hours later, after a 260-mile flight from Posen, the plane landed at an advanced airfield near the headquarters of XIII Infantry Corps. The corps commander, Lieutenant General Erich Jaschke, escorted Bock to a large war map and summarized the first hours of fighting in the corps area. Jaschke was in high spirits; his infantry troops were surging across the Bug at predesignated places and were beginning to invest Brest-Litovsk.

From Jaschke's headquarters, Bock drove by automobile to Guderian's forward command post at Bokhaly, a small village overlooking the Bug about ten miles northwest of Brest-Litovsk. Guderian's chief of staff, Colonel Kurt Freiherr von Liebenstein, was on hand to greet Bock. He told Bock that Guderian had himself crossed the Bug several hours earlier with the vanguard of the 18th Panzer Division. Bock then drove to Lemelsen's command post, located a few miles away at Mukhavetz. In contrast to earlier, optimistic reports, he found that Lemelsen had become agitated and concerned. Russian resistance was negligible, Lemelsen told Bock. Indeed Russian border guards and soldiers were fleeing in panic before the advancing armored columns and the dive bombers. But Lemelsen had just received word by radio from Guderian that the roads on the Russian side of the Bug were fast becoming so soft and marshy that they could not support the weight of the tanks, and Guderian had ordered the tanks and motorized columns to be rerouted across a bridge farther southward at Koden. The bridge at Koden was an ancient wooden one that would have to be reinforced to support the tanks. At that moment, Lemelsen declared, he was waiting for his engineers to either reinforce the bridge or span the river with floating bridge equipment. Meanwhile, the ten thousand wheeled and tracked vehicles of two armored divisions in his panzer corps were converging on the new crossing and a heavy, unpleasant traffic congestion had developed there within the past half-hour.

Bock conferred with Guderian by radio, ate a hasty lunch

with Lemelsen and their aides-de-camp, and then drove to the new crossing site at Koden. When the officers arrived about mid-afternoon, Bock was pleased that German soldiers had met their first test of ingenuity in the German-Russian war. The tanks were already thundering across the hastily strengthened wooden bridge. Lemelsen's engineers had worked frantically to render the bridge usable, sparing their floating bridge equipment for future use. Having accomplished their task, the engineer soldiers stood by, tired, half-naked and water-soaked, but beaming proudly at the immense columns of moving vehicles.[1]

Bock stood by the roadside and watched, too, as the perspiring, oil-stained, dust-covered tank crewmen rattled and roared past. Only the drivers sat inside. The crews rode on top, and the tank commanders stood in their turrets with helmets and headphones. Paraphernalia of all kinds dangled from the sides of the tanks—cooking utensils, water cans, sacks of rations, fuel containers, extra track links, even wooden boards and timbers to be used as matting on the marshy roads ahead.

Some of the tank crewmen, recognizing their field marshal, saluted as they clattered along. The tanks halted intermittently because of the congestion at the bridge. Von Bock stepped onto the road and spoke to a lieutenant standing in the open turret of his tank. The young officer stiffened to attention. In response to von Bock's questions, he said that he was a tank company commander, that his men were in high spirits and his equipment in excellent condition, and that he had fought as a tank commander in Poland and France. "Fine! Hurry up now and get over the bridge so that we can have a clear road," said von Bock.

"Yes, sir!" At the lieutenant's signal the tanks began to move forward.[2]

Bock spent the night in Lemelsen's command post.

"Everything is going according to plan," he noted in his diary. "Russian resistance is light, but it is too early to say if the Russians have put into effect their prepared defense plans. From the reports of all organizations in the army group I get this singular impression: the Russians have been caught by surprise."[3]

They were indeed surprised. In fact, the Russians on that first day of the German-Russian war apparently could not bring themselves to believe that the Germans were invading their territory and intended to destroy them by military force in a blitzkrieg campaign. But toward evening there were signs that they were beginning to recover. As Bock was noting his observations, the unfortunate, harassed Russian General Pavlov, commanding the West Front facing von Bock, was at that same moment issuing orders to the Third, Tenth, Thirteenth, Sixteenth, and Twentieth Armies to immediately counterattack Hoth's and Guderian's advanced positions.[4]

Early on the second day of the invasion Bock crossed the Bug just south of Brest-Litovsk and, escorted by the commander of the 29th Infantry Division, Major General Gustav Schmidt, made his way forward to one of the division's company command posts. Through binoculars he observed the effect of German artillery fire on the Russian bunkers in the fortress city. The Russians were still stubbornly holding Brest-Litovsk, even though German tanks were already thrusting deep into the Russian interior, miles beyond the city. Bock noted with satisfaction that the Russians were responding to the German artillery barrage with only isolated machine gun and sniper fire. "Keep pounding them," he told Schmidt. "They will have to give up soon."[5]

That evening, as Bock read reports from his commanders, he noted that Russian resistance was stiffening everywhere in front of Army Group Center.

Some of my units have captured women prisoners. They [the Russians] are already throwing women into battle, forcing them to hold positions until we either kill them or capture them. . . . What an awful way to fight a war! They will resort to anything to stop our progress! And what a desolate, primitive countryside this is! The people are frightened and shocked beyond belief. . . . We must do whatever we can to alleviate their indescribably deplorable conditions![6]

Bock noted also that evening that although Guderian was having difficulty on the southern flank, Hoth, by contrast, was advancing almost unimpeded through the Baltic states and White Russia. Hoth's northernmost elements had reached the suburbs of Vilna; his southern wing of tanks was approaching Novogrodek, well over one hundred miles from the German-Russian border. This brought up the old question, one which von Bock had not been able to resolve to his satisfaction with Army High Command during the long, methodical preparations and numerous discussions that had preceded the invasion. Should Hoth now turn his main forces southward to encircle Minsk, or should he continue his advance eastward in the direction of Moscow, setting Vitebsk as his next intermediate terrain objective? "I am in favor of the latter course," Bock confided to his diary. "The envelopment of Minsk is not decisive. Besides, I am sure that the enemy expects us to attack Minsk, the next natural objective, and will concentrate defense forces there. . . ."[7]

The attack had gone well during those first two days. The armored breakthroughs at the Russian border, upon which much was staked, were showing signs of being spectacularly successful. At the rate the troops were advancing in those first hours, it was not unreasonable to assume that this would be indeed a blitzkrieg campaign. The Russians surely could be expected to offer sustained battle before long, but for the moment they were disorganized and confused. Bock realized, naturally, that it was imperative to keep them that way if the war were to be won quickly.

Still he was reluctant to instigate more unpleasantness between himself and Army High Command by deciding independently to send Hoth due eastward. Russian soldiers by the hundreds of thousands had been bypassed and were in the process of being encircled, and independent actions on his part to disregard these potentially strong enemy forces might generate nervousness at Army High Command. Bock therefore decided to query Army Commander-in-Chief Brauchitsch on the matter before dispatching instructions to Hoth.

He experienced difficulty in contacting Brauchitsch by telephone from his forward position near Brest-Litovsk, so he talked to Halder. Halder agreed with Bock's calculations, but hesitated to commit himself fully. Finally, after several hours of waiting, Bock heard from Brauchitsch and obtained concurrence in the decision to order Hoth on to Vitebsk.[8]

Bock was gratified that Brauchitsch had finally agreed with him, and he hoped that this portended better relations with his superior officer. He hoped that he would have a free hand in future situations regarding the deployment of his enormous forces. Already Bock's eyes were set on the high ground that constituted the gateway to Smolensk. And beyond Smolensk was the high road to Moscow.

But his satisfaction was short-lived. The war in Russia would be a war of movement, of envelopment, of encirclements, of battles to the death. It would be a war in which the situation changed rapidly and unexpectedly. In one hour operations would go well; in the next, dangerous threats would develop from every quarter to alter drastically what had appeared to be satisfactory progress.

Bock ran head-on into such a situation on 25 June, the

third day of the war. The situation contained three important elements. All three were unpleasant.

First, Hitler received word that Bock had ordered Hoth's armor to advance far into Soviet Russia toward the Vitebsk-Polotsk area. He immediately overruled Bock and sent his personal adjutant, Schmundt, to tell him to concentrate on destruction of huge Russian forces caught in the encirclements north and east of Minsk.

Secondly, Russian troops were beginning to make determined attempts to break out of Hoth's huge pincers between Grodno and Novogrodek and Guderian's between Brest-Litovsk and Minsk. These attempts were disorganized and uncoordinated, but the Russian soldiers were full of fight. Many had not as yet seen a German soldier, but they had suffered the demoralizing effects of German dive-bombing and long-range artillery fire. Orders from their commanders to fight *eastward* did nothing to alleviate their demoralization. Nonetheless, they were ready to engage the German invaders and to repel them at the cost of their lives.

Thirdly, Russian soldiers who were not yet caught in the pincers were counterattacking Guderian's exposed southeastern flank. The counterattacks were far better organized than the desperate breakout attempts. They were led by an officer who would prove to be perhaps the ablest in the Red Army during those early weeks of disaster and retreat, General of the Army I. V. Boldin.[9]

The ferocity with which the Russians fought, even when hopelessly encircled, caused surprise, even consternation, at the German Armed Forces High Command. It was already apparent that the Russians were showing a far greater tenacity than the French and English had done in the Western campaign. This development caused Hitler to become hesitant and cautious.

Von Bock remained, however, unconvinced. He told Schmundt that he opposed the order restricting the movement of his armor, that the infantry should have the mission of "mopping up" the encirclements while the armor continued its eastward drive at all costs. Specifically, Bock opposed turning his armored forces northward and southward to seal the great "pockets" in which the Russians were trapped. He wanted to advance due eastward. If Hitler and the officers at the Armed Forces High Command wanted to exploit the encirclements, he asked Schmundt, why not attempt a larger and even more decisive encirclement farther eastward beyond the Duna-Dnieper River basins? Why not concentrate on Smolensk, the gateway to Moscow? Was not the basic mission to annihilate the enemy before he retreated into the vast interior of Russia? What better way to do that than to keep him off balance by advancing rapidly eastward?

Schmundt then tried to counsel with Hitler by telephone regarding Bock's statements and questions. Hitler could not be reached at that moment, so Schmundt talked to Colonel General Jodl at Hitler's field headquarters, the Wolf's Lair.[10] Jodl advised Schmundt to return but first to tell Bock that a final decision would be forthcoming from Hitler that afternoon.

After Schmundt left, Bock called his army commanders, Kluge and Strauss, and told them to make every effort to seal off the Russians in the encirclements around Grodno, Bialystok, Minsk, and Novogrodek, so as to indicate to Hitler and the Armed Forces High Command that this could be done without slowing down the armor. Kluge was reluctant and told Bock that the counterattacks on his right flank were mounting in intensity, that perhaps he would have to use armor that was earmarked for eastward advances to repel them. Bock wondered aloud to Kluge: "Now, whose side are you on?"[11]

Late that afternoon of 25 June came the decision from Army High Command. The order to Bock was signed by

Brauchitsch, who had apparently been in contact with Hitler since Schmundt's visit. It forbade further advances by the armored forces until the "pockets" were cleared of Russians.

Von Bock raged in bitter frustration. "We are permitting our greatest chance of success to escape us by this restriction placed upon my armor!"[12] Nevertheless, he heeded Brauchitsch's order and accordingly instructed his staff to issue directives countermanding those previously issued.

Late that night of 25 June, Bock's Army Group Center headquarters completed its displacement forward from Posen to Kobryn, an undamaged Russian town about fifteen miles northeast of the fallen citadel of Brest-Litovsk.

On the next day, Brauchitsch flew to Bock's new headquarters. Still very much aggravated at having been overruled, Bock greeted the army commander-in-chief coldly, even when Brauchitsch extended congratulations for Army Group Center's successes to date. Bock was unimpressed. "If you insist on issuing instructions such as those of yesterday," he told Brauchitsch, "I cannot guarantee that the successes will continue."[13] Bock's unrelenting attitude made it easier for Brauchitsch to mention the main purpose of his visit, which, he apparently realized, would result in even more opposition from Bock. He told Bock that Army High Command, acting upon Hitler's wishes, proposed to place both Guderian's and Hoth's armored groups under Kluge's Fourth Army. The armored groups had been operating directly under Bock's command. Further, Brauchitsch stated, infantry units now in Kluge's Fourth Army were to be placed under Weichs' Second Army.

Not unexpectedly, Bock disagreed, and he demanded to know what tactical principles of warfare guided Army High Command. Brauchitsch merely repeated that it was Hitler's instructions. In the end Bock yielded as he had often done previously, and Kluge became commander of the armored groups. Within a short time after Brauchitsch departed, Bock, apparently to relieve his frustration, began a three-day inspection tour of his troops who were fighting over the vast Russian countryside.

> In blistering heat, blinding dust and over frightfully bad roads, I travel mile after mile to my troop units. The soldiers are impressive in their performance. Despite many hardships their morale is high. The supply situation is working well; there is thus far surprisingly little difficulty with the railroads. At VII Corps, where I stopped today, the commander there sees signs of enemy deterioration in his sector. At least that is good news![14]

On the last day of June, elements of the Fourth and Ninth Armies met each other in the area around Slonim, closing a huge trap on thousands of Russian soldiers. As impressive as was this achievement, Bock was concerned that many more thousands of Russians had managed to escape the German pincers and were surging eastward. Accordingly, he issued a directive to his armies immediately to disengage from the encirclement and to prepare once more to drive eastward. The directive permitted the troops forty-eight hours in which to make mechanical repairs.[15]

Once again Bock's decision caused a confrontation between him and Brauchitsch. By telephone Brauchitsch demanded to know if Bock's forces were in fact prepared to advance eastward, and whether or not sufficient forces could be left behind to contain the encircled Russians. Bock firmly but somewhat cynically assured Brauchitsch that the situation was under control. Moreover, Bock added, to hermetically seal the Russians in the encirclements was impractical if not impossible, because of the immensity of the geographical area, with its forests, swamps, rivers, and indescribably bad road networks. Therefore, the best thing to do was to continue the eastward advance.

EARLY   SUCCESSES   AND   FRUSTRATION   57

A few hours later Halder called Bock. Hitler was arriving soon and wanted a comprehensive summary of the situation in Bock's army group. What reports and recommendations did Bock care to make to the Führer? Unhesitatingly, Bock presented his views to Halder. First, Army High Command should not issue instructions directly to his armies, especially the armored forces, without his knowledge and concurrence. Secondly, the threat of a serious Russian breakout in the encircled areas was diminishing rapidly, and neither the Führer nor the High Command need be concerned. Thirdly, the Russians were on the verge of a decisive defeat in the area of Army Group Center. Regarding the last statement, Halder replied that Hitler was certain to be skeptical, and what evidence did Bock have to support it?[16]

"Read the reports from my headquarters!" Bock retorted. "We have already captured over 100,000 prisoners and enormous amounts of enemy supplies and equipment. More prisoners are coming in by the hour. Has the Führer been given access to the very latest information? Your communique today listed less than half of the prisoners we have actually captured!"[17]

By 3 July, Bock's forces were again underway in their drive eastward. In the evening Guderian's tanks crossed the Beresina and Hoth's tanks forced their way across the Duna between Polotsk and Vitebsk. This particular day, the twelfth of the German-Russian war, marked the longest march in a single day by the tanks under Bock's overall command. They covered more than one hundred miles. Bock ordered them to continue their advance and to disregard or refer to him for interpretation any instructions to the contrary that they might receive, from either Army High Command or their immediate commander, Kluge.

Early on the morning of 6 July, Bock received reports that the Russians were concentrating armored forces northwest of Gomel, possibly for a counterattack against the flanks of the fast-moving tank columns. The reports were disconcerting, and Bock speculated that the Armed Forces High Command would become, as was its custom, overly cautious and extremely nervous when it learned of the Russian concentration and impending counterattack.[18] He therefore decided to reconnoiter the area from the air to see for himself the extent of the danger. In his private plane, escorted by fighter planes from Kesselring's Air Fleet 2, Bock flew over the area for several hours, maintaining radio contact with the tank commanders on the ground below. One or two Russian fighter aircraft circled ominously in the distance, but Bock's escort chased them away. He saw at first hand that the Russians were indeed striking hard at Guderian's exposed positions on the ground, but Guderian assured him that there was no reason for undue alarm. On the return flight to his headquarters, Bock flew over the vast territory stretching from Bialystok to Minsk, in which thousands of Russian soldiers had been trapped. From his vantage point in the air he could see endless columns of Russian soldiers fleeing eastward and southward from Minsk. This concerned him for the moment more than the fighting around Gomel, and he immediately dispatched orders to Weichs, commander of the Second Army, to make a determined effort to prevent the enemy soldiers from escaping.

On 7 July, Guderian's tanks crossed the Dnieper River, the last great barrier before Smolensk. Bock was pleased with this progress. But then on the next morning he received a report that Guderian had withdrawn again to the westward side of the Dnieper. Bock immediately sent an inquiry to Guderian and learned that Kluge had ordered the withdrawal. Furthermore, the "unauthorized crossing of the Dnieper," as Kluge termed it, had incited a hefty argument between Kluge and Guderian. Bock defended Guderian, in this particular instance, and ordered the tanks to recross the Dnieper. He then called up Army High Command, again protested vigorously the placing of the armored forces under Kluge's command and demanded that they be returned to his control. The protest availed nothing.[19]

Following his usual procedure when thwarted by Army High Command, Bock left soon afterward by plane on an inspection tour. His destination was Hoth's headquarters, far to the north. There he conferred with Hoth, Strauss, and Lieutenant General Wolfram Freiherr von Richthofen, son of the famed German ace in the First World War and now commander of Air Corps IV which was furnishing air support to Hoth's armored attacks. Again Bock found his visits to the fighting units far more satisfying than the constant wrangling with Army High Command. "Hoth is making good progress," he noted. "He has a vivid picture of the situation. I am especially pleased with the fine cooperation that exists between him and Richthofen. . . . I have instructed him to invest Smolensk as soon as possible."[20]

Returning to his headquarters, Bock felt encouraged, and on that evening of 8 July he issued a resounding order of the day to his far-flung, hard-fighting soldiers.

SOLDIERS OF ARMY GROUP CENTER!

The multiple battles for Bialystok, Novogrodek, and Minsk are concluded. In these battles Army Group Center has engaged four Russian armies, comprising thirty-two rifle divisions, eight tank divisions, three cavalry divisions, and six mechanized brigades.

Of these forces Army Group Center has destroyed twenty-two rifle divisions, seven tank divisions, and all of the enemy's mechanized and cavalry divisions. The enemy's losses are stupendous. They number the following:

287,704 prisoners, including an army commander and several corps and division commanders.

2,585 tanks.   1,449 heavy guns.   346 aircraft.

Colossal amounts of war materiel—small arms, munitions, transport vehicles of all descriptions, and military supplies.

Our own losses are no greater than brave troops are prepared to absorb. You have been victorious against a bitterly fighting enemy, an enemy fighting in many instances to the last man.

I thank you for your loyalty and valor! I thank you for your unflagging devotion and service to the Fatherland!

To the commanders and troops of Army Group Center I hail your untiring efforts and your magnificent achievements!

To the Luftwaffe, which is ever ready to support and to secure us in the air, I express a special word of gratitude!

I know that the Army Group will continue to achieve great success. Let us not rest on our laurels.

We will pursue the enemy relentlessly!

On now to final victory!

> *Long Live the Führer!*
>
> Bock
> *Field Marshal*[21]

During the next days, Bock's proclamation was read to the more than one million soldiers of Army Group Center.

Not all of the soldiers, however, received the order of the day with an outburst of enthusiasm.

In the lonely, endless Russian forest between Minsk and the Beresina River, three weary, footsore soldiers stood stiffly at attention as their company commander, Lieutenant Rudolf Weinrich, read von Bock's ringing words. The soldiers were members of an elite regiment, the 78th Grenadier. They were all from Porz-on-the-Rhine, a small suburb of Cologne. They had known each other since childhood and they had marched and fought in the same unit through Poland, Belgium, Holland, and France. Only one, Kurt Zechler, would survive the long four years of marching and fighting in Russia. The company commander dismissed the formation, and the three soldiers trudged back to their foxholes. They discussed their supreme commander, the man who controlled their destiny.

"Old Feddy is a great strategist," said one, "probably as great as Adolf. I should think that if he has his way, this war will be soon won."

"*Ja*, and I should think his boots fit better than these fit my sore feet," said the second.

"Of course they do," the third soldier added. "Feddy wears green, gold, and blue parakeets on his shoulders and plucks the feathers from them to line his boots!"

"Shh! Here comes the sergeant!" And the three soldiers busied themselves with cleaning their machine pistols.[22]

Such was the attitude of many soldiers who fought for Germany and for Bock in the vast reaches of Russia.

The last weeks of July and early August marked the most spectacular successes made by Army Group Center during the German campaign in Russia. The successes were achieved at tremendous effort by Bock's officers and men and at heavy costs in lives and machines. They were achieved in spite of Hitler's direct interference in the operations and in spite of continuous disputes over tactics between

Bock and Army High Command and between Bock and his subordinate senior commanders—Kluge, Strauss, Guderian, and Hoth, the generals whose duty it was to execute Bock's instructions.

During this period Army Group Center's enormous forces lunged forward into the depth of the Russian land mass, sometimes in vast pincer movements, sometimes by direct frontal thrusts. In the process they forced their way across numerous rivers and streams, one of the most difficult operations in modern warfare. They fought over seemingly endless terrain, through seemingly unlimited forests, over dusty roads and trails when the Russian summer weather was hot and dry, and through mud and mire when summer thunderstorms turned the ground into what seemed a bottomless bog.

They killed or captured thousands of Russian soldiers and destroyed dozens of Red Army units. The period saw the German blitzkrieg at its best.

It is an amazing feature of the German-Russian war, and a tribute to the German field soldier, that he was able to do so much under such adverse conditions and in the face of terrible, often unknown and seemingly insurmountable odds. Time and again the officers and men of Army Group Center received contradictory or countermanding instructions. Time and again the hundreds of thousands of tank crewmen, riflemen, cavalrymen, truck drivers, couriers, communications men, and artillerymen who constituted Army Group Center were given dangerous missions, and they performed them to the utmost of their ability.

Bock remained in close touch with his far-flung units. On 11 July, the cumbersome headquarters of Army Group Center, with its large staff of officers, personnel clerks, communications clerks and large stocks of equipment and supplies moved forward to an abandoned sanatorium in Borissov, a Russian town situated on the Beresina River about fifty miles northeast of Minsk. Bock commented cynically to his chief of staff, Greiffenberg, that the new headquarters adjoined a captured airfield which the Russians had bombed several times within past days, and therefore he was not entirely "receptive to the idea of being greeted by Russian bombs."[23] Greiffenberg told his commander that this was the only suitable location for the headquarters that could be found in that vicinity. When Bock saw that all twenty rooms in the sanatorium had a wash basin and running water he relented in his criticism.

On the next day, anti-aircraft units consigned to the protection of headquarters, Army Group Center shot down a Russian bomber and captured the pilot alive. Bock found the time to have the pilot brought before him. The Russian pilot was the first enemy officer to whom Bock had talked since the start of the invasion. The Russian pilot, Colonel Vasili Semenovsky, apparently awed but still seething with hatred of the Germans, even as he stood in Bock's presence, stated that the Russian military authorities had ordered an attack in the area around Smolensk and that the German invaders were to be driven back at all costs. In his arrogant manner Bock told the pilot that Russian counterattacks were futile, that the German forces had come to Russia to liberate the Russian people from the manacles of Communism. Nevertheless, after the captured Russian pilot had been taken away, Bock alerted his commanders to be prepared to repel any Russian counterattacks on their flanks, for he was privately concerned with the stiffening Russian resistance in the entire area.[24]

On 13 July, in his usual daily telephone discussions with Army High Command, Bock learned that Hitler planned to divert the focus of the German attack into the Ukraine after the capture of Smolensk. This information startled Bock; it was his first indication that Army Group Center would be assigned a secondary role in the German-Russian campaign. Bock was not amenable to this sign of a major change in strategy.

As soon as he could reach Brauchitsch by telephone he inquired about the matter, and there began what would be a long series of protests extending over the next two months.

The principles of modern warfare impel us to adhere to our original plan and to drive eastward toward Moscow. We have defeated great numbers of the enemy, but my intelligence reports indicate that Russian divisions are preparing to stand and fight in the Smolensk-Orsha area. We have the momentum. A decisive victory over the enemy is imminent. I want to finish off the enemy who is concentrated in front of my army group; therefore, I cannot and will not comply with any order to move my forces to the south for the simple reason that I am ordering them to drive eastward.[25]

Brauchitsch reminded Bock that Russian forces were still fighting between the Beresina and the Dnieper and that it was a dangerous venture to drive precariously eastward before these forces were totally destroyed. For the time being, both officers permitted the matter to rest without reaching an agreement.[26]

On the evening of 16 July, Bock's 29th Motorized Division reported that it had entered Smolensk and had captured intact the railroad bridge across the Dnieper River in that key city. Bock was gratified. Early the next morning the Japanese ambassador to Berlin, General Oshima, visited Bock's headquarters and found him in an almost jubilant mood. Bock escorted his visitor on a tour of the fighting front, which included a luncheon at Kluge's Fourth Army Headquarters. When Bock returned to Borissov that evening, he issued instructions that required Weichs to move infantry units of the Second Army across the Dnieper without delay.

Now began a confrontation with Guderian that would

continue throughout the remainder of the campaign. The underlying reason for enmity between these two men stemmed not from disagreement over military tactics, but from a clash of personalities, which dated back to the Austrian *Anschluss* of 1938. Bock was arrogant and zealous of his prerogatives as commander of a huge military force; Guderian was just as arrogant and zealous of his reputation as the "father of the German armored corps." Guderian tended persistently to disregard Bock's instructions and to act independently in his position as commander of Panzer Group 2. While this tendency was also prevalent in Bock's own actions in relationship with his superiors, he resented it in subordinate officers.

The particular event that precipitated the renewal of hostility between Bock and Guderian was the latter's stubborn determination to attack Yelna, a strongly defended Russian town approximately seventy miles east of Smolensk. Bock had ordered Guderian to encircle Smolensk and to meet elements of Hoth's Panzer Group 3 in the area east of Smolensk. Guderian's action, if carried out, would permit thousands of Russian soldiers to escape through the gap that would be left open in the encirclement and would endanger the entire operation. Bock was not, however, opposed to Guderian's proposed attack in principle. He objected to Guderian's lack of consideration for higher authority. He decided to write a personal letter to Guderian.

My dear Guderian:

      You will have to be more reasonable and more cognizant of Army Group Center's requirements. An eastward advance at this particular time is not in accord with my instructions. You will turn the bulk of your forces to the north, as previously instructed, in order to establish contact with Hoth. Upon conclusion of this mission you will be given further orders.

My viewpoint is that the enemy can be more decisively defeated by encircling him east of Smolensk. In addition, you must anticipate that the enemy will probably attack
your flanks and thereby cause a dangerous situation for both
Army Group Center and your own forces.

Bock[27]

By the time Guderian received the letter, his forces had
already overcome resistance in Yelna; however, he turned
northward to make contact with Hoth.[28]

In the midst of Bock's preoccupation with rapid developments in the Smolensk area, he was forced to turn his attention to the problems arising in the areas that had already
been occupied by his army group. On 22 July the rear area
commander for Army Group Center, Lieutenant General
Kurt von Schenckendorff, came to Borissov to visit Bock.
Schenckendorff reported that while activities in the occupied area were generally under control, there were indications that the Russians were resorting increasingly to
guerrilla warfare. Schenckendorff had brought a report prepared by his intelligence officer. The report was based upon
a captured Russian document.

The partisan movement must play a mighty role in our
patriotic war. . . . The basic objectives in the rear areas of the
enemy have been clearly stated by the Chairman of the State
Committee for Defense, Comrade Stalin: "Partisan units
mounted and on foot will be formed at once. Diversionist groups
will be organized to fight the enemy everywhere, to blow up
bridges, destroy roads, damage telephone and telegraph lines,
set fire to forests, stores, and transports. In the occupied regions
conditions will be made unbearable for the Fascist invader and
all his accomplices. They will be hounded and annihilated at
every step and all their measures will be frustrated." . . . The
basic operating unit of the partisans will be the company and
the platoon. Their basic duty will be to attack columns and

concentrations of the enemy's infantry, his storage dumps and ammunition transports. . . . Partisan operations will be carried out as a rule at night and from ambush; they will use forests for cover. . . . Partisans will concentrate on the killing of enemy officers, the burning of enemy armored vehicles by incendiary bombs, and the spreading of rumors designed to produce panic among the enemy invaders. . . .

For the Commander of the West Front
Sobechikov

20 July 1941   *Brigadier General*[29]

Schenckendorff stressed that although the guerrilla attacks on German supply columns and facilities were minor so far, he was concerned that they would increase in intensity.

Bock studied the information carefully. He told Schenckendorff:

Partisan warfare has one basis—hatred. Therefore we must exert every effort to persuade the Russian people to work with us voluntarily. I am sure that this can be done with success on the farmlands by restoring private land ownership to the people. . . . We already have had success with the reintroduction of Sundays and the reopening of churches in the occupied cities and towns.[30]

Bock instructed Schenckendorff to instigate, within the limits of his authority, a program of pacification to diminish the danger of partisan warfare. At the same time, he ordered the combat units to treat Russian civilians sternly but fairly.

During the next days Bock busied himself with getting his infantry across the Dnieper. Weichs' Second Army was hesitant, and Guderian's armored forces showed, in Bock's estimation, too much intrepidity. Both factors caused Bock a great deal of irritation. Weichs' hesitation stemmed from fear of increasingly stronger Russian counterattacks on his right flank. Bock told him that this was of no great concern, that it was imperative to move the infantry forward so the troops could support the armored attacks. "I bear the responsibility for the consequences of the Russian counterattacks," he told Weichs.[31] And he insisted that Guderian retard his headlong advance and await replenishment of ammunition and supplies. Both were reaching a dangerously low level.

Under the mounting pressure of conducting this enormous operation, Bock began to revert to his older approach to principles of warfare. He became cautious and at times even hesitant, and this, in turn, led to a tendency to discredit the blitzkrieg that Guderian persisted in using.

The constant interference by Army High Command with Bock's operation added to his irritation. On 25 July, Greiffenberg returned from a conference with Halder and reported that considerable dissatisfaction with Bock prevailed at Army High Command because of Bock's "uncompromising, uncooperative attitude." Bock wrote in his diary:

This is pure nonsense. My concern is that Army High Command will not split up my army group into three segments. There are rumors afloat that I must send units to the north to help Leeb and units to the south to help Rundstedt and still carry out my mission, but with reduced forces. I trust that Army High Command will forego such a tactically unsound move. If the officers at Army High Command persist, however, they will learn the true meaning of "uncompromising attitude."[32]

On that same evening Hitler made a personal long-distance telephone call to Bock and demanded to know why the encirclement east of Smolensk had not been closed and what Bock's intentions were regarding the Russian counterattacks on Army Group Center's southern flank?

I summarized the situation for the Führer and included all details that I felt he could calmly accept. Nonetheless, the Führer became excited and accused me of not exerting sufficient effort to seal the Smolensk encirclement. He reminded me that Hoth's forces were in a position to do this. I promised the Führer that Smolensk would be completely encircled within a few days, but I was concerned about Guderian's southern flank.[33]

On the next day Bock received a letter from Guderian. The letter accused Bock of disparaging him with Hitler and with Army High Command. Guderian stated bluntly that if Bock was dissatisfied with his leadership he wished to be relieved from command. Bock dispatched an immediate denial to Guderian and told him that he, Bock, did not take kindly to accusations that had no foundation.[34]

Meanwhile, Hitler, who apparently was dissatisfied with the information that Bock had given him in the telephone conversation of 25 July, sent Keitel to Bock's headquarters at Borissov on the morning of 26 July. The discussions between Bock and Keitel were not unpleasant, but the two men reached no tacit agreement. Keitel informed Bock of Hitler's deep concern over the fact that Bock was formulating his own strategy rather than executing the mission assigned to Army Group Center. This mission, Keitel reminded Bock, was to encircle and destroy the enemy where he stood. Bock replied that this was being done, but also it was a mistake to attempt completely to seal each and every small pocket of enemy resistance. If higher authority persisted in such demands the achievement of the final objective would be indefinitely retarded.[35]

On 27 July, Hoth's forces, advancing southward, made contact with Guderian's units and finally sealed the huge pocket around Smolensk. During the next hours Russian attempts to break out of the pocket reached great intensity. In the vicinity of Gomel, Russian divisions attacked Guderian's right flank. Acceding to Hitler's demands, Bock ordered Guderian to turn elements of his armored group southwestward to destroy the Russian forces that were making these determined counterattacks. Guderian was reluctant and flew to Bock's headquarters to protest the new order. "We are supposed to be advancing towards Moscow," he told Bock. "What is the sense of attacking backward in the direction of our homeland?"[36] Guderian's protests availed him nothing, and he proceeded to carry out the instructions.

Having settled this issue at least temporarily, Bock turned his attention once again to the rear areas of the army group. Persistent reports indicated that Russian partisan activity was increasing. Russian stragglers and partisans were destroying railroads, attacking supply columns, and overrunning small guard detachments far behind the front. There were reports of fighting even in the occupied areas west of Minsk. Bock dispatched instructions to Schenckendorff, commander of the rear area, "to correct the situation at once."[37] Back came a request from Schenckendorff for more troops to deal with the partisans. Reluctantly Bock assigned the 161st Infantry Division, a combat unit, to Schenckendorff's command. "I do this with a heavy heart," said Bock, "because I need the division on the front lines."[38]

The dual responsibility of overseeing the areas occupied by his troops and the conduct of combat operations bore heavily upon Bock. He had never implemented Hitler's infamous and controversial "political commissar order" in his army group. He seemed to believe sincerely that the role of the German Army in the invasion of Soviet Russia was not only to destroy the Soviet Armed Forces, but to rid the Russian people of Communism. His repeated attempts to clarify or to modify Army High Command's policy with regard to the treatment of Russian civilians and military stragglers had not resulted in any changes to his satisfaction. He regretted that much disagreement and difference of viewpoint regarding the occupied areas existed between him and the higher authorities. He does not seem, however, to have placed the final responsibility for the steady increase in Russian guerrilla activity upon Hitler, who had ordered the Russians to be treated severely. This remains inexplicable.

In an effort to come to closer grips with the problem of partisan warfare, Bock ordered his intelligence staff to prepare a report of the partisan situation. The report was completed in the second week of August. It claimed that:

> The Russian partisan movement is receiving its greatest strength from stragglers and escaped prisoners of war. Most of these are passing as natives of the local villages and towns which have been occupied by Army Group Center. . . . Indications are that most of the stragglers do not wish to go on fighting. . . . The situation is one of extreme confusion.

> It is urgently recommended, first, that new identification credentials be issued to every Russian civilian. Secondly, those Russian soldiers who have attempted to integrate themselves peacefully with the community must be assisted in finding employment. Thirdly, those Russian soldiers who persist in fighting must be captured as early as possible and interned as prisoners of war.[39]

The report also recommended that harsh measures be taken against those captured soldiers who had attempted to conceal their identity or who had partaken in partisan activities. Bock approved the recommendations and ordered them to be implemented. Accordingly, intelligence officers in Army Group Center prepared thousands of leaflets to be dropped by air over Army Group Center's occupied areas during the following weeks.

The leaflet stated:

SOLDIERS OF THE RED ARMY!

Your commissars are forcing you to remain in the forests,
to terrorize the population, to burn houses and crops, and
to attack German soldiers. What will you do when you have
plundered the villages and the countryside and winter comes?

Come to us voluntarily before it is too late. You will
receive bread and work. After the war you will be permitted
to return to your homes. Do not persist in futile partisan
warfare. Report to the nearest German military unit at once
and you will be treated as bonafide prisoners of war![40]

Bock's program met with only partial success. It is impossible to state exactly how many encircled Red Army
soldiers read the leaflets. The result was that during the
following weeks many surrendered, but thousands more
continued to roam about the countryside, raiding and am-
bushing German march columns, isolated units, and supply
lines.

On 1 August Bock received a startling memorandum
from Army High Command. The memorandum directed
Army Group Center to prepare for a probable commitment
of its forces to the Russian Ukraine. The memorandum be-
wildered Bock. "What," he asked Army High Command,
"has become of the initial plan? Are we to give the enemy
an opportunity to build a new front before Moscow?"[41] He
received no clear answers to his inquiries.

On that same day Guderian reported that Yelna had been
captured and that his advance units were within sight of
Vyasma. Hoth, likewise, reported that his tanks had bypassed Yarsev and were advancing against little or no resistance toward Sitshcheva. Moscow was less than 200 miles
away.

On 2 August Keitel telephoned Bock from the Wolf's
Lair. Hitler, stated Keitel, would arrive at Borissov on 4
August for a firsthand look at the situation in Army Group

Center's area. Bock was optimistic, despite the disconcerting memorandum that he had received earlier about a possible diversion of his forces to the south. He had not seen Hitler for several months. He was in a good mood when Hitler and his personal adjutant, Schmundt, arrived at the Borissov airfield. "The Führer greeted me pleasantly," he stated later, "and congratulated me on my army group's successes, which, he stated repeatedly, are 'reshaping world history!'"[42]

Soon after Hitler's arrival at Borissov, Bock's optimism faded. He discerned that Hitler, despite his enthusiasm, was unsure about the future prosecution of the war. Bock had instructed his armored commanders, Hoth and Guderian, to be present, and he had advised them to impress upon Hitler the fact that it was most imperative to continue the advance to Moscow. Further, Bock stated, he would support their viewpoint. For reasons that remain inexplicable, in view of the importance of Hitler's visit to Army Group Center, Bock had not required his army commanders, Kluge, Strauss, and Weichs, to be present.

To Bock's perplexed disappointment, the conference that he confidently expected did not take place. Instead, the astute Hitler, ever ready to play a guessing game with his generals, even when he himself was uncertain about future operations, talked individually to each officer. While Hoth and Guderian waited in an anteroom, Bock summarized the general situation for Hitler. He ended by pointing out the urgent importance of maintaining pressure on the retreating Red Army and of continuing the attack directly to Moscow. Hitler listened attentively. When Bock finished, Hitler asked abruptly: "When do you estimate that your forces will be in Moscow?"

Without hesitation, Bock answered: "By the end of August."[43]

After similar private discussions with Guderian and Hoth, Hitler summoned all three officers and spoke at length about general strategy. He told them that it was important for Germany to conquer the Ukraine and the Crimea. But he did not commit himself regarding the continued advance to Moscow.

The discussion then turned to technical details, such as tank replacements for Hoth's and Guderian's commands, and the havoc that the Russian dusty roads had played with both men and machines. During these technical discussions, Bock chose to remain silent and to await Hitler's expected approval of the continuation of the advance to Moscow. But the approval did not come. After about two hours at Borissov, Hitler departed rather abruptly. He had not clarified the situation at all and Bock was puzzled about Hitler's intentions.

Hitler's visit to Borissov on 4 August was a turning point in the German campaign in Russia. On that decisive day Bock lost an opportunity—his last opportunity—to influence the conduct of the war. Bock could have conferred with Hitler from a position of strength. His forces had been the most successful of the three army groups that had launched the invasion of Russia. Bock's losses of 74,000 had been the heaviest. But in just six weeks, Army Group Center had advanced over 450 miles into Soviet Russia and had destroyed or captured vast numbers of the Red Army. While Bock had not succeeded in destroying the entire Red Army that confronted him within the allotted time previously envisaged in Operation *Barbarossa,* the fact was that the Russians were in precipitate retreat. Under Bock's relentless prodding, Army Group Center had outgunned, outmaneuvered, and outfought the Red Army. The road to Moscow lay open.

In those early August days, Bock stood perhaps at the pinnacle of his military power. He would never reach that peak again. By submitting to Hitler's tactics of conferring individually with each officer, Bock permitted Hitler to outwit him. It is probable that, had Bock exacted an approval from Hitler to continue the eastward advance, he could have indeed entered Moscow in triumph by the end of August. Whether or not the capture of Moscow in the summer of 1941 would have meant complete victory for Germany over Soviet Russia is a question that military historians will long debate. Russian historians of the Second World War, which they refer to as the Great Patriotic War for the Fatherland, concede that the Red Army's defenses on the West Front facing Bock had broken down, but that "heroic resistance had forced the Fascist invaders, led by Bock's Army Group Center, to revert to a war of defense."[44] In conceding the disintegration of their defenses, however, the Russians also tacitly admit that at the current rate of advance the German forces could have conquered Moscow. Still the questions remain. With the loss of Moscow, would the Soviet Russian government have surrendered? Or, would the soldiers and people of Soviet Russia have continued to resist the German invasion from areas deep within their land mass, from the Urals, and from behind the Volga?

Hitler's visit to Bock on 4 August exposes, also, the glaring lack of cooperation and perhaps enmity that existed between Army Group Center and Army High Command. During the visit, Army High Command had hastily dispatched a minor officer to the Borissov conference as its representative. Why did not the commander-in-chief, Brauchitsch, attend the meeting? Or, perhaps, the chief of the general staff, Halder? Or, a senior staff officer, a general? The meeting was important; the future conduct of the war rested upon what Bock and his commanders told Hitler and upon what decisions Hitler would now make. Both Brauchitsch and Halder favored a continuation of the advance to Moscow and the destruction of the enemy forces facing Army Group Center. Did they trust Bock to persuade the wavering Hitler without their support? Or did they *distrust* him and therefore leave him to his own devices in his confrontation with Hitler?[45]

On 5 August, Bock issued another order of the day, his second of the German-Russian war. The document had been prepared before Hitler's arrival.

SOLDIERS OF ARMY GROUP CENTER!

With the destruction of the last Russian divisions in the Smolensk encirclement, the great battles which have been waged for weeks along the Dnieper and Duna Rivers are now concluded. They have resulted in a brilliant victory for German arms!

Again the soldiers of Germany and of Army Group Center have fulfilled gloriously their duties!

During the course of these battles, Army Group Center has captured or destroyed:

309,110 prisoners of war.   3,205 tanks.
3,005 heavy artillery pieces.   341 aircraft.

Enormous amounts of enemy supplies, equipment, and vehicles of all description, which are at this moment still being counted.

I hail your accomplishments with gratitude and pride!

I hail your bravery, your valor, and your unswerving devotion to our Fatherland!

Your accomplishments belong to history!

Long live the Führer!

Bock
Field Marshal[46]

On that same day, at the regular conference at Army High Command, Halder suggested to Brauchitsch that an attempt should be made to clarify for the army group commanders the major objectives of the German-Russian campaign. Apparently concerned about Hitler's increasing tendency to interfere in the tactical operations, Halder noted that the high leadership was busying itself with too many details that were the concern of the field commanders.

It would be far better to determine once and for all what objectives the political leadership [Hitler] intends to attain. If
for economic reasons we are to conquer the Ukraine and the
Caucasus, then let it be made clear that the major objective
cannot be the destruction of the enemy's military forces. If the
major objective is Moscow [and the Volga], then it cannot be
the Ukraine. Above all, let us have clarity and freedom of
operation.[47]

But the situation was not clarified. Instead, it degenerated
in those August days into a state of vacillation and confusion
that may have cost Germany the war. Acting apparently
upon the assumption that Hitler and the Army High Command would give *ex post facto* approval to his operations,
Bock pressed the advance eastward towards Moscow. By
mid-August, Guderian's armor had driven to a considerable
distance east of Roslavl and had gained control of the
Smolensk-Moscow highway. Despite strong enemy counterattacks from a southerly direction and the ever-present
problem of ammunition and fuel shortages, Bock's troops
were in an almost jubilant mood. Their goal was almost
within reach. Traffic control units erected signs along the
highway. The signs all pointed eastward and read: "To
Moscow—160 miles."[48]

To the north, Hoth's armor, which had had easier going
than Guderian's from the very beginning of the invasion,
drove a wedge between Velikiye Luki and the marshy headwaters of the Duna. On 14 August Hoth's reconnaissance
elements reported that they were within sight of Rshev on
the Upper Volga. From Rshev to Moscow the distance was
about 100 miles. The almost complete absence of Red
Army concentrations on Hoth's front caused Bock to become suspicious. At his request, Kesselring's reconnaissance
aircraft flew numerous missions over the desolate forested
area east and southeast of Rshev. They reported that no significant Russian military activity could be observed. The

highways and byways leading to Moscow were undefended.

In a long, coded report to Army High Command, Bock reported that Army Group Center's mission was on the verge of full accomplishment. Guderian and Hoth had captured still another large number of prisoners, about 75,000, and vast amounts of Russian war materi 1. On the next day, Bock informed Army High Command, he expected that Guderian would cross the Oka River between Yukhnov and Kaluga and that Hoth would probably reach Volokolamsk.

Army High Command's reply to Bock's long report was laconic and vague. Bock simply could not understand why the officers at Army High Command did not share his enthusiasm. "There are too many conditional factors, too many suppositions, in everything they say," Bock noted. "Why do they not see that victory is within our grasp? One really wonders who holds the reins of responsibility at high headquarters. All they have to do is give us freedom of movement and the necessary supplies, then sit back and wait. Instead, the nearer to victory we come, the more funereal they seem to be."[49]

Bock was soon to discover the cause of the funereal atmosphere at Army High Command. Early on the morning of 16 August, he received a teletyped order. The order bluntly directed Bock to transfer four divisions from Hoth's armored group to Army Group North. With a cold fury born of total incomprehension of such an unexpected move, Bock argued long and stubbornly with Brauchitsch over the telephone. "How can you justify such action at this time?" Bock wanted to know. "Do you not realize that you are weakening my forces at a most crucial moment? If Leeb must have reinforcements, why not get them from France? Or Norway? Or the Balkans? My army group is approaching Moscow; do you not see that it is of utmost importance that I retain every man and every vehicle?"[50]

Almost sadly, Brauchitsch tried to placate the infuriated Bock. But he intimated that these transfers of Bock's divisions were only a beginning, and that in the very near future more transfer orders would be forthcoming.

During the evening Bock read situation reports from Guderian's armored group and from Weichs' Second Army. Large Red Army concentrations had been observed in the area south of Gomel, and Red Army units were beginning to mount increasingly intense attacks against the exposed southern flank of his army group. The reports added to Bock's worries.

On 18 August, Army High Command ordered Bock to divert Guderian's armor to the south, presumably to ward off the danger of the Russian counterattacks. The order stated that Guderian was running the risk of a disruption in his lines and would therefore attack Klini and Novosibkov at once to secure the situation. When Guderian received the order from Kluge, his immediate superior officer, he protested not to Kluge but directly to Bock. He told Bock that he could not comply with the order, because he had already instructed his armor to advance towards Moscow. The two men lost their composure and argued furiously. Bock, the angrier of the two, explained in outraged tones that he himself had not originated the order, but that he had no recourse but to issue it, because it had come from Army High Command. Guderian stated that to divert his forces southward he would have to commit all of his reserve units, which he had been saving for the final lunge at Moscow.

On that same day, 18 August, a long conference took place at Hitler's headquarters, far back in East Prussia. The conference was to have a profound effect upon the future course of the war. As usual, Hitler's intuitive strategy took precedence over the more practical and perhaps more nearsighted suggestions of the German professional officers.

On 21 August, Armed Forces High Command issued top-secret Directive No. 34, signed by Hitler. The fateful die was cast. Army High Command received the directive on 22 August and forwarded it to Army Group Center without comment.

The directive stated in part:

The suggestion made by the Army on 18 August with regard to the further prosecution of the war in the east does not meet with my approval.

I order herewith the following:

1. The most important objective before the onset of winter will not be the conquest of Moscow, but the investment of the Crimea, the industrial and coal-producing areas of the Donets Basin, and the Russian oil-producing areas in the Caucasus, and, in the north, the isolation of Leningrad and the establishment of a conjunction with the Finns. . . .

3. Army Group Center will, regardless of planned operations, release the necessary units to accomplish this objective, which hinges upon the destruction of the Soviet Fifth Army. Army Group Center will adopt a position of defense and will utilize only those units that are necessary to repel enemy attacks on its front. . . .

5. Only when Army Group South has destroyed Russian divisions on its front, and only when Army Group North has closed the encirclement of Leningrad and made contact with the Finns, will Army Group Center renew the attack. Its mission will then be to successfully engage and destroy the enemy before its front. . . .

Adolf Hitler[51]

When Bock read the directive, a feeling of deep depression seized him. He sat for a long time at his desk in the confiscated Russian sanatorium in Borissov, the headquarters of Army Group Center. Then he began to pace the floor.

What has happened to the sanity at Armed Forces High Command, he asked himself? They have taken victory away from Germany and from me, a victory that was so close at hand. How is it possible that they do not see their mistake?

Is it possible that they have misunderstood, or misinterpreted, my own statements? This war is unmatched in history in its hugeness and scope. It has ramifications that will be felt by future generations. Is it possible that Armed Forces High Command will prove incapable of conducting such an enormous and historically important military operation?

It is significant that Bock did not place the blame for this fateful turn of events upon Hitler but upon the leadership at the high headquarters.

Finally his depression and bewilderment changed to anger and determination. "I must do whatever possible to prevent the perpetration of this great mistake," he noted.[52] Even as he prepared himself to do this, another telegraphed order arrived from Army High Command. Army Group Center was required at once to release XII and XIII Corps and all subordinate units, including the 1st Cavalry Division, to the command of Army Group South. Eventually, the order stated, all armored and motorized divisions then assigned to Army Group Center would be transferred until further notice to Army Group South.

Bock determined to protest the order. While his staff officers prepared to implement the order, he contacted his commander-in-chief, Brauchitsch, by long-distance telephone. There followed a long, heated discussion.

Bock: I am releasing the organizations in my command according to your instructions. I hope this will prove to be satisfactory. But I will tell you that all of this is, in my professional opinion, quite asinine. It has come to my attention that your headquarters believes that my objective is the capture of Moscow. This is untrue! My first objective is, and has been, to destroy the enemy forces, after which Moscow will fall into our hands like a ripe cherry! There is, then, only one solution on my front. Attack the enemy! Defense is absolutely out of the question! How can you expect me to repel the enemy with weakened forces? And, by the way, how long will this transfer of forces from my army group be effective? Every hour that we lose is irretrievable. We are permitting the enemy the time he needs to recover, to slip from the noose we have placed upon him. There is no doubt that the enemy will now strengthen his resistance and reorganize his defense, as he has been trying to do since the campaign began!

Brauchitsch: I understand all that. Your remarks are quite clear. You will understand, however, that I did not make the decision.

Bock: I am sure of that. But I repeat: a change in tactics at this time is disastrous.

Brauchitsch: If the order to release your forces for the southern operation had not been issued, would you have been in a position to attack eastward without reinforcements?

Bock: Certainly.

Brauchitsch: What armored forces do you need to continue the eastward advance?

Bock: Exactly those that I have been ordered to give up.

Brauchitsch: Can you hold your front without them?

Bock: Not very long.

Brauchitsch: Can you hold for eight days?

Bock: Probably for eight days, but not longer. I emphasize that we are "cutting off our noses," no matter how long or how short a time we are required to defend our front. I request herewith that new decisions be made with regard to the military operation.

Brauchitsch: I am not sure that this will be done. The question is whether or not we can do the best we can in the present circumstances.

Bock: Well, I propose to continue the attack with my remaining forces. . . .[53]

A few hours later, still more telegraphed orders arrived at Army Group Center. "The 10th, the 17th, and 18th Panzer Divisions, the 29th Motorized Division, and the 134th, 167th, and 260th Infantry Divisions are transferred at once to the command of Army Group South," the order stated. "Colonel General Guderian will command this contingent."[54]

With great reluctance, Bock approved the transmission of the order to the divisions concerned. Later in the evening he called Guderian and ordered him to report to Army Group Center by noon of the next day.

This fateful change of military operations had immediate repercussions throughout Bock's enormous command area. One example was the 18th Panzer Division, one of the elite units. Far to the east of Bock's headquarters, the hardened veterans of the division were bivouacked not far from the banks of the Desna River, about fifty miles east of Roslavl and about 150 miles west of the Soviet Russian capital, Moscow. The veterans had fought under Bock for two years. Most of them thought that they understood their commander's whims. Earlier on that afternoon of 22 August, the tank battalions of the division had been alerted for a crossing of the Desna. The crossing would follow an artillery bombardment at 4:00 A. M. on the next morning. Enemy resistance was expected to be "negligible."

In one of the tank battalions, four crewmen of a Mark IV tank loitered around their vehicle, eating a meal of *Zwieback* and canned beef. A few days before, one of their colleagues, the fifth crewman, had been killed by a Russian sniper's bullet, fired from a supposedly abandoned farm house, not far from the Roslavl-Moscow highway. The German tankmen felt deeply the loss of their dead colleague, and they discussed him in hushed tones. But this was war, a very tough war. And despite their grief they also felt a sense of good fortune. That afternoon they had received a new track for their tank. They had refueled and lubricated the tank and had received a surprisingly plentiful supply of ammunition.

Soon one of the four was called away for guard duty. Shortly afterward, the platoon sergeant approached the remaining three who sat idly near their monstrous vehicle. His name was Paul Krueger. He had been a soldier in the German Army since 1934 and had been assigned to the *Panzerkorps* since 1937. His home was Bayreuth, and he had once wanted to be a musician.

Krueger looked puzzled and his voice was crisp.

"Orders have been changed," he told the tank crewmen. "We will not cross the Desna tomorrow morning. Instead, we will reconnoiter the area due south of us in the direction of Novgorod. We depart at 3:00 A. M. Do you understand?"

"Yes, Sergeant," replied one of the crewmen. "But may I ask, are we not to go ahead to Moscow? That is to the east. Why are we advancing southward? Will we have the pleasure of shooting up Ivan in the South before we have the pleasure of seeing the Kremlin?"

"I issue orders," said Sergeant Krueger. "I do not explain them. All I know is the orders are from the highest authority. If you want an explanation, consult our almighty Feddy von Bock. I am sure he has one!"[55]

And the soldiers wondered if their commander, Bock, had actually agreed to the drastic change of operations.

On the afternoon of 23 August, Halder flew to Borissov. Halder spent an hour with Bock, explaining the justification for the change in the operations. He then told Guderian, who was also present, that in all likelihood Hitler would require his presence at the Wolf's Lair on the next day. Bock wondered why he was not also required to be present. After Halder departed, he and Guderian conferred at length about possible developments. Despite the personal enmity that existed between the two officers, neither found it difficult to agree that the change of tactics was unwise, and that the best possible chance of success was to continue the eastward advance. Bock impressed upon Guderian the importance of defending this stand during the conference with Hitler.

Upon his return from the conference Guderian stopped at Borissov to tell Bock that "the decision to veer southward had already been made and that all the protests were to no avail."[56] Again Bock was infuriated with Guderian. "That really finishes him with me," he wrote in his diary. "It simply proves that he has no loyalty and is too easily persuaded. . . ."[57]

During the next days Bock tried to continue the attack toward Moscow with his depleted forces. For this he depended upon the infantrymen of the Second, Fourth, and Ninth Armies. Since most of their armored and motorized equipment had been transferred to the Ukraine, they made little progress, though there was little Russian resistance. On 31 August, Bock received an order from Army High Command that instructed him to make no further advances to Moscow until he received clear authorization.

Early in September, Army Group Center established headquarters in the eastern sector of Smolensk. From this new headquarters, Bock continued, in spite of instructions to the contrary, to conduct local attacks against the enemy, though in considerably lesser scope than those of the past weeks before Directive No. 34 had been issued.

On 9 September, Army High Command asked Bock to prepare an operation order for the continuation of the attack to Moscow. The attack would be given the code name Operation *Typhoon* and would begin at the latest on 30 September. Bock supervised carefully the preparation of the new operation with his staff, adding more details than he wanted to, but hoping that by doing so he would for once satisfy Army High Command. A few days later Army

High Command telegraphed its approval of the operation order. It also informed Bock that, beginning in mid-September, Army Group Center would be reinforced and replenished with men and vehicles. Its composition would be three infantry armies, the Second, Fourth, and Ninth which had been originally assigned, and three tank armies, the Second, Third, and Fourth. The Second and Third Panzer Armies were outgrowths of Hoth's and Guderian's original Panzer Groups; the Fourth Panzer Army, commanded by Colonel General Erich Hoepner, had hitherto been assigned to Army Group North.

Thus when Operation *Typhoon* began, Bock had stronger forces than those with which he had started the campaign. They totaled almost one and a half million men, including many battle-tested veterans of the heavy, costly campaign in Russia. The news that his force would once again be authorized to renew the attack led Bock to forget all of the frustrations and disappointments of the past weeks.

Meanwhile, the operation in the Ukraine had been very successful. By mid-September, the great battle of Kiev was almost over, the Russian Fifth Army and elements of two others had been destroyed, and almost 700,000 prisoners of war had been captured.

Between 22 and 28 September, Bock occupied himself with inspection tours of his reinforced Army Group Center. Accompanied by Kesselring, he flew several times over the Russian countryside, ranging far into enemy territory. On one occasion, Bock and Kesselring, guarded by fast fighter planes, flew over the city of Moscow. Bock saw that the Russians had erected formidable fortifications in a semicircular fashion in front of Moscow. He also noted that the fortifications had not been there in late July and early August.

On 29 September, Bock held a conference of his senior commanders, Strauss, Hoth, Kluge, Weichs, Hoepner, Guderian, and Kesselring. The conference had an atmosphere of grim determination rather than confidence. The optimism of earlier days was gone. Bock, however, drove home his point. Moscow must be taken by 7 November, before the onset of Russian winter. Besides, he had promised Hitler that Moscow would be in German hands by that date.

After the conference had ended and Bock's commanders had departed for their respective field headquarters, Bock sat down and wrote an order of the day.

SOLDIERS OF ARMY GROUP CENTER!

After weeks of waiting, the army group renews the attack!

Our objectives are none other than the destruction of remaining enemy forces to the east of us and the capture of the citadel of Bolshevism—Moscow!

I am confident that you will perform your duties as faithfully and bravely as you have done in the past!

Let us not falter! Let us march to final victory in this war!

Bock
Field Marshal[58]

Early on the morning of 30 September, Hoth's, Guderian's, and Hoepner's armored forces, following a devastating air and artillery bombardment, began to convege on Moscow. By 2 October, the Second, Fourth, and Ninth Armies were in motion. Bock followed the progress of the enormous force on his great war map.

The distance from his most advanced units to Moscow was less than 100 miles. And Bock saw no reason why Army Group Center could not enter the city in three or four weeks.

1. The information in these paragraphs is taken from H. Gp. Mitte KTB, microfilm no. 220/65002/30/490-497 (Washington, D.C.: U.S. National Archives n.d.).

2. Germany, 1952. Personal interview with Karl-Heinz Bernsdorff, a former German soldier.

3. Von Bock KTB, 22 June 1941.

4. P. A. Shilin, *Vazhneishie Operatzii Veliki Otchestvennoi Voini* (Moscow, 1956), p. 93.

5. H. Gp. Mitte KTB, microfilm no. 220/65002/30/499 (Washington, D.C.: U.S. National Archives, n.d.).

6. Von Bock KTB, 23 June 1941.   7. *Ibid.*, 24 June 1941.

8. H. Gp. Mitte KTB, microfilm no. 221/65002/39/615-16 (Washington, D.C.: U.S. National Archives, n.d.).

9. Shilin, p. 96.

10. The Wolf's Lair was located in a heavily wooded, stringently secured area near the East Prussian town of Rastenburg, about 450 miles northeast of Berlin. Hitler maintained his headquarters there from the start of the Russian campaign until the last months of the Second World War.

11. Von Bock KTB, 25 June 1941.   12. *Ibid.* 13. 26 June 1941.

14. *Ibid.*, 29 June 1941.

15. H. Gp. Mitte, microfilm no. 220/65002/30/501 (Washington, D.C.: U.S. National Archives, n.d.).

16. Halder KTB, III, 30 June 1941, p. 29, and von Bock KTB, same date.

17. Von Bock KTB, 30 June 1941. The date was also Halder's birthday, and Halder devotes considerable space in his diary to telling of the congratulations and presents that he received from his staff, from the Armed Forces High Command, from Hitler, and even a telephone call from Frau von Brauchitsch, wife of the army's commander-in-chief. Halder does not mention the verbal altercation with Bock in his diary; neither does von Bock mention that it was Halder's birthday in his. See Halder KTB, III, 30 June 1941, pp. 30–31.

18. Russian concentrations in the Gomel area did indeed become a source of concern at Army High Command and in both Army Groups

Center and South. See Halder KTB, III, 6 July 1941, pp. 34–35, and von Bock KTB, 7 July 1941.

19. Von Bock KTB, 7 July 1941.

20. *Ibid.*, 8 July 1941.   21. *Ibid.*

22. Germany, 1949. Personal interview with a former soldier of the Wehrmacht.

23. Von Bock KTB, 11 July 1941.

24. H. Gp. Mitte KTB, microfilm no. 215/26974/23/997 (Washington, D.C.: U.S. National Archives, n.d.). This is a prisoner-of-war interrogation report.

25. Von Bock KTB, 13 July 1941.   26. *Ibid.*   27. 18 July 1941.

28. Guderian, p. 164.

29. Earl Ziemke, "The Soviet Partisan Movement in 1941" (Washington, D.C.: Air Research and Development Command, U.S. Air Force, 1954), pp. 14–16.

30. Von Bock KTB, 22 July 1941.   31. *Ibid.*, 23 July 1941.

32. *Ibid.*, 25 July 1941.   33. *Ibid.*

34. *Ibid.*, 26 July 1941. Guderian does not mention the letter in his memoirs.   35. *Ibid.*

36. Guderian, p. 165.

37. H. Gp. Mitte KTB, microfilm no. 215/8755/15/654–56 (Washington, D.C.: U.S. National Archives, n.d.).

38. Von Bock KTB, 28 July 1941.

39. H. Gp. Mitte KTB, microfilm no. 215/8755/15/678 (Washington, D.C.: U.S. National Archives, n.d.).

40. *Ibid.*, microfilm no. 215/8755/15/703–704.

41. Von Bock KTB, 2 August 1941.   42. *Ibid.*, 3 August 1941.

43. *Ibid.*, 4 August 1941. Bock states that Guderian was present, but the latter mentions only that he flew alone to Hitler's headquarters on 2 August in an effort to have the Ukranian engagement rescinded. See Guderian, pp. 180–81.

44. Shilin, p. 157.

45. Halder is noncommittal about Hitler's conference at Army Group Center on 4 August. Although Halder favored a continuation of the eastward advance, as did Bock, he is quite critical of Bock during the period. One entry in Halder's diary refers to Bock as irresponsible or frivolous. See Halder KTB, III, 4 August 1941, p. 155.

46. Von Bock KTB, 6 August 1941.

47. Halder KTB, III, 5–6 August 1941, pp. 155–57.

48. Guderian, who spent much time with his forward units writes that he viewed the scene with a "painful heart," a statement that apparently is made in retrospect. Guderian seems not to have surmised at that time that the advance to Moscow was going to be delayed because of Hitler's change of strategy. See Guderian, p. 167. There is little doubt, however, that the German soldiers of the advance armored units confidently expected to be in Moscow within weeks.

49. Von Bock KTB, 14 August 1941.   50. *Ibid.,* 16 August 1941.

51. Hitler's Directive No. 34 is quoted in Halder KTB, III, 22 August 1941, pp. 192–93; in Tippelskirch, p. 230; in Hubatsch, p. 188; in Trevor-Roper, p. 90; and in Walter Warlimont, *Im Hauptquartier der deutschen Wehrmacht: 1939–1945* (Frankfurt, 1962), p. 205.

52. Von Bock KTB, 22 August 1941.   53. *Ibid.*   54. *Ibid.*

55. Germany, 1950. Personal interview with a former soldier of the Wehrmacht.

56. Von Bock KTB, 24 August 1941. Guderian claims that the high officers who were present at the conference, including Keitel, Jodl, and others, supported Hitler and that he, Guderian, stood alone in his urgent requests to Hitler not to change the scope of the operations. See Guderian, p. 180.

57. Von Bock KTB, 24 August 1941.   58. *Ibid.,* 29 September 1941.

IV. "THE LAST BATTALION WILL DECIDE THE ISSUE!"

EARLY ON THE

morning of 30 September 1941, Field Marshal von Bock's three panzer armies launched a tremendous attack on the Russian defenses guarding the approaches to Moscow. From the south and northwest, endless columns of German vehicles roared and rumbled across the rugged countryside on a front more than four hundred miles wide. The weather was perfect; the sun shone with the golden pallor of a Russian autumn. German Stukas and low-flying bombers struck ahead of the advancing columns, bombing Russian defenses, known troop concentrations, airfields, towns, and cities. Every German soldier and airman in the land and air armada of Army Group Center knew what was expected. Moscow must be taken while the good weather lasted.

Each man knew, too, that the task would not be easy. The Russians had shown far more capacity for fighting than had the forces of western and southeastern Europe in earlier blitzkrieg campaigns. Moreover, during the weeks since late August, when Hitler had ordered Army Group Center to fight a defensive engagement, the Russians had brought more troops into the areas between Smolensk and Moscow and had constructed formidable defenses. When Bock's attack began, Army Group Center faced the Russian Third, Tenth, Thirteenth, and Twentieth Armies, plus major elements of at least four others. Their combined strength was greater than Bock's forces, perhaps two times as great.

In preparation for the assault, the Russians employed every conceivable device, every conceivable method of defense known in modern warfare. In the most likely avenues of the German armored attacks, they had emplaced tanks and artillery in the ground, so that the gun barrels protruded inches above the earth's surface. They had laid thousands of mines, many of which were crude and homemade but effective, in the paths of the German vehicles. As defense against the German infantry, they had strewn more thousands of anti-personnel mines and ingenious booby traps, all set to explode and kill or maim at the touch of a man's foot.[1] Along the roads leading to Moscow, and in their towns and cities, the Russians had erected sandbag, log, and heavy barbed wire barricades. These were manned by Russian soldiers—and often civilians—who knew that the penalty for desertion was death.[2]

And now, as Bock's attack got under way, the Russians saturated the area with millions of high-explosive shells. In some instances, fanatic defenders strapped explosives around their bodies and threw themselves under the advancing German tanks. In other instances, they fastened explosives on the backs of unfortunate dogs, which had been trained to dash upon command under the nearest German tank. All along the front the Russians brought out their new, truck-mounted multiple rocket launchers, which would prove to be one of the deadlier defense weapons of the Second World War. The rocket launchers fired salvos of large-caliber shells ranging up to 400 millimeters at a rapid rate. Bock's soldiers quickly named these weapons *Stalinorgel.*[3]

The first days of October 1941 witnessed some of the most bitter fighting in the Second World War. But despite the Russians' determined resistance, it soon became apparent that the sheer weight and ferocity of Bock's attack had caught the Russians by surprise, as had happened three and a half months earlier when the invasion began. Their surprise was due, mainly, to the very short time it had taken Bock's forces to concentrate and deploy for the assault. This, in turn, had been due in large part to Bock's insistent prodding. Since mid-September, Bock had stressed the necessity for haste. In oral and written instructions and on inspection tours to his subordinate armies, corps, and divisions, Bock had emphasized that speed and surprise were the main elements of the new assault. Although Bock had concerned himself with manpower problems, he had devoted particular attention to the enormously difficult supply situation that faced Army Group Center, and he had directed a complete rejuvenation of the supply and transportation system in his vast, complex command. Bock's staff officers had estimated that Army Group Center would require daily thirty trainloads of supplies and 1500 tons of fuel, once the attack was underway.[4] To insure that these colossal amounts would be forthcoming, Bock had conferred frequently with Army Commander-in-Chief, Field Marshal von Brauchitsch, with Chief of the General Staff, Colonel General Halder, and with Quartermaster General of the German Army, Colonel General Eduard Wagner.

To the southwest, Guderian's Second Panzer Army, now reinforced with Lieutenant General Werner Kempf's XLVIII Panzer Corps and several motorized and infantry divisions from Army Group South, attacked in a northeasterly direction, with two important rail and highway centers, Orel and Bryansk, as intermediate objectives. Throughout late August and most of September, Guderian's armor had played a leading role in the great battles of encirclement and destruction of Russian forces around Kiev. In late September, when Bock ordered Guderian to envelop Moscow from the southwest, Guderian not only had the difficult task of reorganizing, replenishing, and deploying his scattered, depleted divisions, but he also had the longest distance to travel. Guderian had vigorously opposed Bock's decision to attack on 30 September, stating that since only fifty of the promised three hundred new tanks and about half of the required fuel supplies had arrived in his army, he could not be ready to attack on that date. But Bock had been adamant, and Guderian had duly set his tanks in motion on the morning of 30 September.[5]

Turning to the northeast meant exposing Guderian's right flank to disorganized but stubbornly fighting Russian units in the Orel-Kursk sector. It also meant a widening of the gap between Guderian's right flaık and the northernmost elements of Rundstedt's Army Group South. This development concerned Bock far more than Guderian's complaints about the shortage of tanks. It had long been the subject of heated discussions between him and Army High Command. Bock had maintained throughout the Russian campaign, perhaps quite rightly, that it was a gross tactical error for Army Group South to veer away into the vastness of the Russian Ukraine and Donets Basin, leaving Russian forces free to concentrate in the Orel-Dimitrovsk-Kursk-Byelogorod areas and thus pose a threat to both his right and Army Group South's northern flanks. But Bock's protests had been overridden. So now he considered that at this late date alternatives were too few, and the exposure of Guderian's right flank was just another of the risks that had to be taken.

On 1 October, Guderian's XXIV Panzer Corps, commanded by Lieutenant General Leo Freiherr Geyr von Schweppenberg, broke through Russian resistance at Svesk and moved swiftly along the paved highway to Orel.[6] On the same day, Hoepner's Fourth Panzer Army, which had been assigned to Bock's command from Army Group North only a week earlier, crossed the Desna River in the middle sector of Army Group Center's front and gained freedom of movement deep within Russian territory. Hoepner's intermediate objectives were the capture of Kaluga, a sizable town about eighty miles southwest of Moscow, and the encirclement of Russian forces that were known to be concentrated near Vyasma.[7]

Farther to the north, Hoth's Third Panzer Army and its battle-tested veterans of earlier, spectacular successes at Minsk and Smolensk, made a similar breakthrough. One main column of Hoth's tanks struck toward Rshev on the Upper Volga; a second column skirted the headwaters of the Dnieper and headed for Volokolamsk; a third crossed the Dnieper farther south and began to forge the northern pincers of the encirclement at Vyasma.[8]

On the morning of 2 October, the mass of Bock's infantry, comprising the Second, Fourth, and Ninth Armies, went over to the attack. Theirs was the difficult task of maintaining pace with the fast-moving armor. Immediately, all along the front they ran into fierce resistance. The fighting was intense and savage. And as Bock studied his maps and awaited reports on the progress of the fighting, hundreds and hundreds of deadly dramas were taking place far to the east. What follows is one example.

In a forested area a few miles southwest of Yartsevo, which was a sector of Ninth Army's front, Lieutenant Heinz-Otto Krause, a company commander in the 456th Grenadier Regiment, 256th Infantry Division, stood quietly among his men. At exactly 5:40 A. M., 2 October, Krause glanced at his wristwatch and began to speak in a slow, distinct tone:

Attack time is in five minutes. The company's objective is to test the enemy's strength in the forest directly in front. The company will advance in ten single files, with ammunition carriers and heavy machine gunners in the middle. As soon as the Russians begin to fire, each man will attack on the run, firing from the hip. In the event that I am unable to continue, command of the company will pass to Lieutenant Walter von Krüger. If Krüger falls, Sergeant Bergmann assumes command. If Bergmann is unable to command the company, the attack must be halted, and every man will withdraw to the original starting point to await further instructions. I repeat previous instructions: it is strictly forbidden to attend to the wounded or remove the dead. Stragglers will be punished as in the past— by summary execution. Now, good luck to all, and let us have a go at Ivan!

At 5:45 A. M., Krause's men, heavily laden with weapons, equipment, and ammunition, started across the forest. When they had advanced about three hundred yards, the hidden Russians suddenly opened fire. Rifles and machine guns blazed seemingly from behind every tree, from beneath every scrub brush. Mortar shells burst among the crouching Germans.

"Fertigmachen zum Sturm!" bellowed Krause. And every man ran forward at full speed, firing and screaming as he ran. Within minutes German and Russian soldiers were locked in deadly, hand-to-hand combat. Bullets, rifle butts, hand grenades, bayonets, daggers, broken tree limbs, even fists, became the weapons of the desperately struggling men. Some sank silently to the ground, as if felled by a terrific, unseen force. Others staggered and lurched about, screeching in terror and pain. One young German soldier sagged limply against a tree, reluctant to fall, unable to stand. His helmet and weapon were gone; part of his tunic was sheared off. Blood trickled down his blond hair; he stared in disbelief at the gory stump that had once been his right arm.

As suddenly as they had started firing, the Russians broke off the fighting and fled in the direction of Yartsevo, the yelling Germans hard on their heels, firing as fast as they could reload their weapons. Within a quarter of an hour some of Krause's men had reached the eastern edge of the forest. They set up heavy machine guns and fired across a clearing into Yartsevo, less than a mile away. Krause drew his flare pistol and shot a green flare into the air.

Krüger and thirty-seven others of the original 120 men who had begun the assault were missing somewhere in the forest. Krause and Bergmann, breathless and exhausted, their faces grimy, their uniforms in tatters, sat under a birch tree and watched tracer bullets from the machine guns slam into the wooden buildings in Yartsevo, adding fires to those that had been already started by an earlier Stuka bombardment.

Krause ordered an extra ration of schnapps to be passed out to his men. From his pocket he produced a flask, took several deep swallows and handed the flask to Bergmann.

"Well, Bergmann," Krause finally spoke, "Ivan is tough, but if our good luck holds, Adolf will soon be standing atop the Kremlin's walls, with his right arm stretched out over Red Square."

"Yes, *Herr Leutnant,* and I daresay that old Feddy von Bock will be standing there alongside him. Rumor has it that he is more anxious to look down upon Red Square than is Adolf!"[9]

It was perhaps just as well that Bock never knew of these and countless thousands of similar remarks that his soldiers made about him.

At noon of the same day, an order of the day, signed by Adolf Hitler, arrived at Army Group Center. "Soldiers of the Eastern Front! For the past three and a half months everything possible has been done to prepare for this final powerful thrust which will smash the enemy before the onset of winter. . . . Today begins the last decisive battle of the year!"[10]

Late in the evening at his headquarters, Field Marshal von Bock noted in his diary: "The attack is going according to plan all along the army group's front. In fact, my troops are advancing so rapidly that I wonder if the Russians are up to their old tricks and are withdrawing *en masse*."[11] Bock then directed Kesselring to intensify air reconnaissance over the broad approaches to Moscow. On the same evening, Halder also noted in his diary: "Operation *Typhoon* opened this morning in beautiful autumn weather.... It has hit with great force, and everywhere Army Group Center is making pleasurable progress...."[12]

During the first October days, it appeared as if Operation *Typhoon* had been appropriately named. Although Bock had personally supervised the planning and preparation for this "last decisive battle of the year," he had not been consulted in the choice of a code name for the attack. That had been done by Hitler himself. With his usual flair for the dramatic and sensational, Hitler knew that the very term would provide a psychological lift for both the battle-hardened veterans of Army Group Center and the German soldiers and airmen yet untested in the rigors of the merciless Russian campaign, who had been transferred from France, the Balkans, even Norway, to replace Bock's losses. Bock recalled a private conversation with Hitler ten months earlier, in December 1940. As he had lain ill in bed during one of Hitler's visits, he had expressed concern to Hitler that the Russians would fight stubbornly for their capital. But Hitler had impatiently dismissed Bock's concern. "They will think a hurricane has hit them!" had been Hitler's words.[13]

At his headquarters on 2 October, as he read early reports of Army Group Center's advances, Bock reflected that a typhoon and a hurricane were different forces, but then a typhoon could have the same devastating effect as a hurricane—if it hit in the right places.

On 3 October, Hitler addressed the Reichstag in Berlin. In a speech lasting more than two hours amidst much applause and many "Heils!" he recounted in great detail the success that German arms had achieved in Soviet Russia since 21 June 1941. Most of European Russia, almost 100 million people, and over seventy percent of Russia's industry and communication centers, Hitler stated, were now under German control. He concluded with what would turn out to be quite an exaggeration: "Forty-eight hours ago began a battle of gigantic proportions! The enemy is broken and will never rise again!" These words were broadcast by German radio to the whole world.[14]

On the afternoon of 3 October, Guderian's tanks rolled into Orel. From Orel, a paved highway led to Moscow, 180 miles away. The Russians were so surprised by the appearance of the German tanks in the city that the streetcars were still running. They had planned to evacuate industrial machinery from Orel, but had had no time to carry out the evacuation. "All along the streets between the railroad station and the factories lay dismantled machinery, numerous crates of tools, and piles of raw materials, all scattered about in the utmost confusion," Guderian recorded.[15]

On the same afternoon, another powerful column of Guderian's Second Panzer Army, Lemelsen's XLVIII Corps, reported that it had bypassed Bryansk and was nearing Kuraschev. Upon receipt of this news, Bock ordered Guderian to press on to Tula.[16] Within two hours, however, Bock experienced his first disappointment of the renewed attack. Army High Command countermanded Bock's instructions to Guderian and instead directed Guderian to concentrate stronger armored forces in the Bryansk area, where, in conjunction with Hoepner's tank columns advancing from the northwest, a huge encirclement of Russian forces was developing. Bock now had to make a vital decision. Air reconnaissance indicated that the area between Orel and Tula was comparatively free of Russian forces. This meant that possibly within hours Tula would fall to Guderian's tanks with the same relative ease and rapidity as had Orel, provided that Guderian pressed the attack with energy and determination. Tula was an important industrial and railroad center; its fall would most certainly deal a devastating blow to the Russian line of defense south of Moscow.[17]

On the other hand, the prospect of destroying the huge Russian force at Bryansk was enticing. It promised the same kind of spectacular successes that had characterized Army Group Center's campaign during the early weeks of the invasion. Moreover, reports streaming into Bock's headquarters indicated the probability of still another vast encirclement to the north around Vyasma. Hoth's and Hoepner's tanks were ranging far into Russian territory, and it appeared as if their respective southern and northern wings could hem in the Russian forces concentrated between Yartsevo and Vyasma.

Bock weighed the various factors in the crucial situation. He pondered whether or not to ignore Army High Command's countermanding orders to Guderian and instruct him to advance toward Tula, or to accede to Army High Command and concentrate in Bryansk. It was feasible that since Army High Command had seen fit to delay Guderian's forward advance, it would act similarly with regard to Hoth and Hoepner.

After some deliberation, Bock reached a decision. The Bryansk and Vyasma encirclements must be completed, and the Russian forces caught there must be destroyed. Bock then telephoned Guderian and instructed him to direct the necessary tank units northwestward to Bryansk. At the same time, Guderian should attempt to seize Mzensk and Bolkhov, two smaller towns located about forty miles northeast of Orel. He dispatched similar instructions to Hoepner and Hoth with regard to Vyasma.[18]

Bock's decision to accede to Army High Command and

to concentrate on the destruction of Russian forces at Bryansk and at Vyasma, rather than to push rapidly to Moscow, is subject to debate. Earlier, Bock had not been at all reluctant to voice disagreement when he considered that his decisions and actions as commander of a huge, far-flung, complex military force were more valid than those of Army High Command. Why did he not do so this time? Did the possibility of surrounding the Russians and inflicting a severe defeat on them at Bryansk and Vyasma offer too great an attraction? Bock had promised Hitler that his forces would enter Moscow in early November. In past weeks he had stressed the value of time as one of the most important factors in the battle for Moscow. Did he, for the moment, lose sight of this all-important factor? Russian resistance was becoming stiffer and more desperate in some sectors of Bock's front; the Red Air Force had even bombed Orel severely on the same evening that Guderian's forces had captured the city, inflicting casualties on Germans and Russians alike. But there were indications that the Russian front was collapsing and that Bock's armored columns could have been in Moscow by mid-October, well in advance of Bock's timetable. Some Russian historians, in subsequent accounts of this crucial period in their country's history, have conceded this.[19]

In August 1941, Hitler had overruled the recommendations and suggestions of Army High Command, the General Staff, and the senior field commanders—particularly Bock—and had directed the conquest of the Ukraine before the conquest of Moscow. Since that date, Hitler had in name and in fact assumed control of all military operations on the Eastern Front. The army and the professional Officer Corps had been relegated to the role of messengers.[20] Bock was aware that Hitler now made all of the tactical as well as the strategic decisions, and it is probable that he was reluctant to contest Hitler at this point.

It is probable, but not certain. At least two things, however, are fairly certain. First, in his decision Bock considered the interests of himself, the waning prestige of the German Officers Corps, and the welfare of Germany; and second, neither he nor any other man could have foreseen at that moment the calamity that would befall Army Group Center during the next weeks.

On 5 October, Bock boarded his special train and started on an inspection tour of his command. While en route to Fourth Army headquarters he visited briefly several infantry and tank divisions and talked to generals, colonels, noncommissioned officers, and privates. As he took leave of the 7th Infantry Division, one grizzled old sergeant, the veteran of two world wars and dozens of close brushes with death, saluted and said: "We shall soon be in Moscow, *Herr Generalfeldmarschall!*"[21]

At Fourth Army, von Kluge received his commander pleasantly and summarized the situation in his army area. Since Kluge's army occupied the middle sector of Army Group Center's front, Kluge was not confronted with the perennial problem of flank security. He informed Bock that the situation appeared to be optimistic in Fourth Army's area. Bock was pleased that Kluge was in a cooperative mood.[22]

From Fourth Army, Bock traveled to Second Army headquarters, where he discussed the rapidly developing Bryansk encirclement with Second Army's scholarly commander, Freiherr von Weichs. Satisfied that Weichs had sufficient strength to close the Bryansk pocket, Bock directed him to invest Sukhinichy and Byelev at the earliest possible time, opening the way to the important railroad town of Kaluga. After a pleasant dinner at Second Army with Weichs and his higher staff officers, Bock departed aboard his special train. He had learned much about the actual situation during his brief trip, and he had become openly enthusiastic about the Bryansk and Vyasma encirclements. "It will be a great accomplishment," he noted. "I hope our strength and our precious time will not be adversely affected by the 'mopping-up' operations in the pockets."[23]

At Army High Command, Halder noted that "Army Group Center's campaign is proceeding in truly classic fashion. . . . The enemy's resistance varies from place to place, according to the troops at his disposal. But it is evident that he cannot resist much longer. . . ."[24]

On the morning of 6 October, as Bock left his train at Smolensk, he noted that the Russian skies had turned leaden gray and that a cold, sinister wind was blowing from the north. Bock reminded himself that he must have his quartermaster general make inquiries at Army High Command about the promised winter clothing for his troops and antifreeze solution for their vehicles.

At his headquarters, Bock learned that Guderian's 17th Panzer Division had taken Bryansk "with surprising ease," and that the other units of Guderian's forces and those of Hoepner's Fourth Panzer Army had made contact in the vicinity of Khvastnovichy, about sixty miles east to Bryansk. The Bryansk pocket was closed. Divisions of Weichs' Second Army were also closing in on the surrounded Russians. That was good news, but it was the last that Bock had on that day.

Somewhat later a dispatch arrived from Army High Command, directing Bock's dashing commander of the Third Panzer Army, Colonel General Hoth, to be transferred to Army Group South. Replacing Hoth as commander of the Third Panzer Army would be Lieutenant General Georg-Hans Reinhardt, formerly one of Hoth's corps commanders. Reinhardt was a professional tank officer who, along with Guderian, Walter Nehring, Otto von Knobbelsdorf, Ewald von Kleist, Hoepner, and other professional officers had built up the German Army's tank corps during the years preceding the war. He was a highly respected and competent officer, but Bock regretted the change. Hoth was one of the few senior officers under Bock's command with whom Bock had never had a serious disagreement. Although strong-minded with regard to his profession, as most German officers were, Hoth had not tried to impose his own professional analyses upon Bock when there was a divergence, as Kluge, Guderian, and others had done. So Bock called Halder to inquire if Hoth could remain in his command at least until all the highways and roads to Moscow were cleared. Halder demurred, and Hoth duly took leave of Bock's Army Group Center.[25]

On the afternoon of 6 October, a cold rain began to fall on the northern sectors of Army Group Center's front. Within an hour the Russian countryside had turned into a quagmire. Roads became muddy canals; fields and forests became boggy swamps. And the tens of thousands of vehicles in Bock's command became stuck in the mud. Tanks and other tracked vehicles managed to move forward at a snail's pace; truck and other wheeled vehicles were hopelessly mired, despite the efforts of many thousands of men to extract them from the mud. Toward evening the temperature dropped; the rain turned to snow and spread over the entire front.

From his headquarters at Orel, Guderian telephoned Bock to ask about winter clothing and anti-freeze solution, none of which had as yet arrived. The unpleasant change in weather and Guderian's agitated telephone call prompted Bock to fire off a teletyped message to Army High Command. "Where are the winter supplies that you have promised us?" was the gist of the message.[26] A few days were to pass before Bock's headquarters received an answer from Army High Command stating that winter supplies were being shipped to the battlefront. The reply suggested to Bock that if he attended to his responsibilities the supply officers at Army High Command would attend to theirs.[27]

Bock now turned his attention to the Vyasma encirclement in Ninth Army's sector. His intelligence reports estimated that over forty-five Russian divisions, composed of at
least 450,000 men, were concentrated in the Vyasma pocket
that had been formed by Hoth's (now Reinhardt's) Third
Panzer and Hoepner's Fourth Panzer Armies. But since
the tanks could not completely seal off the pocket—only infantry could do that—thousands of Russians were escaping
eastward out of the pocket. Moreover, to Bock's distress,
there were indications that the infantry of Strauss's Ninth
Army was not exerting the effort that Bock thought necessary to liquidate the encirclement. Bock telephoned Strauss
to urge him to greater effort in this important task. A serious
altercation between Bock and Strauss ensued. The rain
and snow had rendered the terrain impassable and movement impossible, Strauss stated heatedly. Additionally, even
if his troops could move with the speed of the past days, it
seemed more feasible to advance toward Borodino, and had
not Bock himself stressed this feasibility in earlier instructions? Furthermore, Strauss concluded, attacks by Russian
partisans were increasing alarmingly in Ninth Army's Rear
Area Command, and these were not only disrupting the
logistical situation, but were causing confusion and disor-
ganization in the combat zone and in the rear. During the
past forty-eight hours, over sixty attacks by partisans on
truck convoys, outposts, and railway lines had been reported.

Neither man was able to convince the other. Finally Bock
lost his temper, reminded Strauss that he, Bock, was the
army group commander and bore responsibility for the
success or failure of the operation, that Strauss had sufficient
security troops to ward off partisan attacks, and that Strauss
would do well to conduct himself and execute his mission
in accordance with his position as an army commander.[28]
On the next day, after considering the incident with Strauss,
Bock wrote Strauss a long letter:

Dear Strauss:

I regret that developments during the past ten days have led to a misunderstanding between us. I am sure that in view of the great successes to come you would have preferred to prevent this, as I do. You are aware that from the very first order that I issued for this attack I have stressed orally and in writing the necessity for the infantry to follow closely the armor and to support it with the greatest energy. This holds true in the case of the Vyasma encirclement.

I am not unaware of the extremely difficult conditions regarding supply, transportation, and communications behind your front. I do not agree, however, with your analysis that it is impossible to move your infantry. I remind you that despite adverse terrain conditions, the infantry in the other armies continues to move forward. It is imperative that we prevent the enemy from breaking out of the Vyasma pocket and reforming his defenses to the east and northeast.

There is sound basis for my previous instructions to you. During the battles at Minsk and at Smolensk, I urged repeatedly that the armor be allowed freedom of movement as soon as possible, to prevent the enemy from regrouping his defenses. This, of necessity, placed a heavy burden on the infantry, but in this campaign it affords the only chance of defeating an enemy who has traditionally used his vast, primitive terrain to his own advantage. . . .

At Minsk and at Smolensk, because of circumstances beyond my control, I was not able to execute this concept of warfare. As a result, both engagements, though successful, were not decisive. *This must not happen again!*

It is my desire that all of us will share in the fruits of impending victory in this eastern campaign. To do this, however, I must enforce my will, even at the risk of endangering the friendly relations that have heretofore existed between us.

I hope that this explanation will bring about a renewal of the comradely cooperation that I have enjoyed with you in the past and that has contributed to many earlier successes by the army group.

Very truly yours,

Bock   *Field Marshal*[29]

During the morning of 7 October, the temperature rose, the snowfall ceased, and by noon the sun shone again over the Russian landscape. The million and a half German soldiers under Bock's command stirred from their makeshift shanties, from their mired vehicles, and, for the more fortunate, from their warm Russian dwellings. They scraped the mud from themselves and their vehicles; cleaned their rifles, machine pistols, and heavy guns; and prayed for the good weather to last.

In the afternoon, Brauchitsch landed at Bock's headquarters aboard his Junkers special plane. Bock reported that both the Bryansk and Vyasma pockets were practically sealed and were being narrowed down, and that it appeared that the greatest prize of the war was in the offing. Brauchitsch was complimentary and profuse with his congratulations. As an aside, he stated: "This time things will be different. This time you will not be inhibited in your conduct of the operations, as at Minsk and Smolensk. . . . This time, Herr Bock, you will have a free hand to drive forward. . . ."

Bock was skeptical.

"Well, I hope so," was his laconic reply.[30]

By morning on 8 October, the ground dried sufficiently to support vehicular movement. Guderian's 17th Panzer Division secured its hold on Bryansk, having moved into the city from the east. His 4th Panzer Division stabbed toward Tula but ran into stiff opposition and was forced to withdraw to its original position northeast of Mzensk. Bock telephoned Guderian and expressed concern over an old problem, the security of Guderian's right flank. Guderian retorted that the situation was under control and that he was adhering to Army Group Center's instructions. Regarding the capture of Bryansk from the east, Guderian would not be denied an opportunity to show his sarcasm and contempt for Army Group Center's conduct of the operations. "In which direction is Moscow?" he asked.[31]

In the north Hoepner's and Reinhardt's tanks seized Vyasma. The German tanks approached from an easterly direction, surprising the Russian defenders. But at both Bryansk and Vyasma the Russians fought viciously to hold open their escape routes. Losses were considerable on both sides. Bock dispatched telegrams to his army commanders, instructing them to address themselves with energy and haste to the task of eliminating the two pockets and to press the attack to Moscow. He asked Kluge to estimate the time of the capture of Borodino and Mozhaisk. Bock's intention was to announce simultaneously the fall of Borodino, the site of Napoleon's great victory in 1812, along with the victories at Bryansk and Vyasma. Borodino was less than sixty miles from Moscow. Kluge replied that with proper armored and air support he could take the historic city within a week.[32]

Late in the evening of 8 October a telegram arrived at Army Group Center from Armed Forces High Command. The telegram was signed by Adolf Hitler. In it, Hitler instructed Bock to place the Third and Fourth Panzer Armies astride the Smolensk-Moscow highway and to envelop Moscow with all possible speed from the north and south. Further, Hitler ordered, Bock should utilize the 19th Panzer Division and the SS-Grenadier Regiment *Grossdeutschland* to prevent the enemy's breakout of the Bryansk pocket. The tone of Hitler's telegram was one of impatience and annoyance. By implication rather than outright statements, he showed dissatisfaction with Bock's progress and hinted that Bock was perhaps permitting himself to be influenced by too many precautionary considerations.[33]

As had often happened earlier in the campaign, Bock was

angered and puzzled. "Just who is conducting this war, anyway?" he asked himself. True to his professional creed and to his long-standing contempt for the officers at higher headquarters, the "arm-chair *Kommandos*," Bock concluded that it was not Hitler, the chief of state, who was at fault, but the terribly incompetent staff officers in Hitler's entourage who were failing to inform Hitler of actual developments.[34]

It seems not to have occurred to Bock that a senior officer in his own command may have bypassed him and appealed directly to the highest authority.

Bock's telegraphed reply was on its way to Hitler within minutes.

Mein Führer! Although some elements of the Third and Fourth Panzer Armies, and the Second as well, are already attacking toward Moscow, other elements of these organizations are now engaged in liquidating the Vyasma and Bryansk pockets. It is, therefore, impossible to commit them fully at this time to an eastward drive. Moreover, they will need the support of the Fourth, Ninth, and Second Armies, and all available air power. The roads are again impassable and are filled with supply columns, for it is essential to bring up fuel and ammunition for the combat forces. The 19th Panzer Division is already past Yukhnov; in view of the heavily congested roads, it is not feasible to turn the division around and direct it to Bryansk. At the moment, I am not aware of the exact location of SS-Grenadier Regiment *Grossdeutschland*.... Request information as to which has priority—SS-Grenadier Regiment *Grossdeutschland,* or fuel and ammunition for an army group?

Bock[35]

On 9 October, after a short respite of good weather, the Russian countryside was again blanketed by rain, sleet, and snow. And again Bock's military machine bogged down. German soldiers shivered in the freezing temperatures and worked with almost superhuman effort to maintain the momentum of the attack. They used horses, machines, and sheer human strength in an attempt to extract their vehicles from the Russian mud. But despite all they could do, the forces of nature proved to be superior, and the Battle of Moscow became the Battle of Mud. Hundreds of abandoned vehicles littered the muddy trails and the swampy fields. Dead Germans could often be seen in or near isolated vehicles, the victims of partisan attacks.[36]

Von Bock made a tour of the northern sector of his front, talked to a number of corps and divisional commanders, and reached the conclusion that despite the adverse weather his men still held a tactical advantage over the Russians. Again he urged the infantry armies to press forward and place themselves between the surrounded Russians in the Bryansk and Vyasma pockets and their escape routes to the east. While returning to his headquarters, Bock learned to his chagrin that the Greater German radio, in one of its special war bulletins which were now blaring forth continuously throughout German-occupied Europe, had announced a great victory at Bryansk.

Bock contacted Halder at Army High Command. "There you go again with your premature announcements," Bock fumed. "Are you not aware of the true situation here? Neither the pocket at Bryansk, nor at Vyasma has as yet been liquidated. But they will be. Meanwhile, kindly refrain from proclaiming victory beforehand."[37]

Bock's protests to Hitler and the Army High Command apparently had results. On 11 October, Army High Command, acting upon instructions from Hitler, addressed a query to Bock. "What is your estimate of the situation, in view of the bad weather? Is it practical to continue the operation?"[38]

Again Bock faced a crucial decision. He felt gratified that, for once, the highest military authority in Germany had seen fit to shoulder him with the responsibility that was rightfully his. But he also felt the heavy weight of his responsibility. He knew that he now stood before the judges of history.

Military perfectionist that he was, Bock considered carefully the factors that could lead him to the proper decision. What was the tactical situation? Were his forces defeating the Russians? All reports from Bock's commanders indicated that although the Russians were fighting stubbornly, even desperately, organized resistance in the conventional military sense was collapsing and the Russians were on the verge of a decisive strategic and tactical defeat. Therefore, the answer to the second question was "yes."

What of his own command? Did the officers and men of Army Group Center possess the necessary combat strength and logistical support not only to inflict a decisive defeat on the Russians but also to exploit it? Were they capable of moving on to Moscow, which in ordinary conditions was a drive of less than two hours by vehicle? In the two weeks since Operation *Typhoon* had begun, Bock's losses in men and equipment had been heavy, but not intolerably so. Since 30 September, Army Group Center had lost about 35,000 men, excluding the sick; about 250 tanks and heavy artillery pieces; and several hundred other vehicles.[39] Most of the tanks and other vehicles had been lost to the muddy terrain during the past forty-eight hours; comparatively few had been lost to enemy action. Supplies, especially fuel and ammunition, were extremely slow in reaching their intended destinations and were hardly adequate. Only about twenty of the thirty trainloads that were required daily were reaching the combat forces. Nevertheless, Bock's supply experts estimated that supply shortages were being compensated by improvisation and expediency among the units. For instance, every vehicle that had to be abandoned to the mud or because of mechanical failure was "cannibalized"; that is, the vehicle was stripped of usable parts and fuel for other vehicles that were still functioning. The lack of winter supplies was thus far the most pressing problem.

The next important factor, more difficult to assess than his own capabilities, or even those of the Russians, was the weather. At the moment, it was creating a graver problem for Bock's forces than were the Russians themselves. The weather technicians in Bock's air force units had made an exhaustive study of the weather in the Moscow area. But technical data were sketchy, for no one in the entire German military hierarchy had taken into account that von Bock's hundreds of thousands of soldiers would be slogging through knee-deep mud on the approaches to Moscow in October 1941. Therefore, the best long-range prediction that could be made was that the rainy or snowy season would continue for another two weeks or so, interspersed perhaps by short, rainless or snowless periods. This would be followed by a period of cold, dry weather, lasting through most of November.

Then there was yet another vital factor to be considered. During the two years since the Second World War began, the Wehrmacht had built up an image of invincibility. The German military machine had thus far ridden roughshod over all of its opponents on the European continent. Every civilized nation, whether German-occupied, allied, belligerent or neutral, had been awed by the Wehrmacht's new concept of warfare, the blitzkrieg, and the convincing victories that it had achieved. Therefore Field Marshal von Bock, proud, haughty and ever the militarist, wished to be the last person on earth to damage or destroy the German Army's aura of invincibility. Moscow was within his grasp; it would probably be never so closely within his grasp again. This was his chance, Bock considered, to add his name to posterity as the conqueror of Moscow.

Finally, there was the very practical consideration that

the forces of Army Group Center had no other place to go, no other alternative but to press the attack. From a purely military standpoint, it was just as difficult to halt the attack operation and attempt to establish a defense line deep inside Russia, 600 miles from their bases of supply, as it was to continue the attack. The difficulties and obstacles that now faced Bock's enormous forces would not be erased by such a move. Indeed, they would increase, because the Russian defending forces would not have been defeated, and the initiative would eventually pass to them.

Having considered all of these factors, both definite and probable, Bock reached a decision. His reply to Army High Command was far simpler than the complicated reckoning that had produced it. "I recommend a continuation of the attack," stated Field Marshal von Bock.[40]

Although large numbers of Russians were trapped at Bryansk and Vyasma, thousands of other Russian soldiers were deployed in the forests that abound north and west of Moscow. These forces and the mud comprised formidable enemies. On 12 October, the Third Panzer Army reported that its units had bypassed Volokolamsk and, after heavy fighting, had cut the Kalinin-Klin highway at a point forty miles due north of Moscow.

A Russian participant in the fighting in the area, Colonel S. N. Sevrugov, a regimental commander in the 53rd Cavalry Division, has described its intensity:

.... The enemy bombarded our position with bombers and fighters, sometimes in groups of one hundred planes or more. The forest (north of Volokolamsk) was filled with the smoke of numerous heavy explosions. Old trees crashed to the earth, the air was very hot and stifling, and it was difficult to breathe....

It was apparent that the enemy intended to envelop us from the southeast. He pressed his attacks with great intensity. His infantrymen were supported by numerous tanks.... Under pressure of superior numbers I ordered my regiment to conduct a fighting retreat.... Our reconnaissance showed that the enemy's motorized columns were moving parallel to the railroad that runs to Klin....

During the night of 11 October, the main elements of my regiment reached the highway just north of Klin. It was cold, wet, and very dark. The Fascist tanks, truck loads of infantry, motorized artillery, and special vehicles of all kinds were advancing southward along the road in an endless stream. Their vehicle motors growled and rumbled; their blacked-out headlights shone dimly in the autumn rains. With great caution, so as not to give an alarm, our squadrons formed into attack units. The stream of Fascist vehicles struggled along and finally disappeared out of sight. There was the silent muddy road, deeply rutted from numerous wheels and tracks. We waited....

Again there came the rumble of many engines and soon more blacked-out lights appeared. Another enemy column was approaching.... On they came—Fascist tanks, trucks, and artillery. Some of the vehicles were towing others and frequently became stuck in the mud. They were so close that we could hear the cursing voices of the poncho-covered soldiers as they pushed the heavy, bogged vehicles through the mud.... I estimated that in another hour it would be daylight....

At the correct moment I gave the command. "Forward! Shoot at the headlights! All squadrons! Charge!"

Gunfire lit the darkness. The vehicles' headlights began to extinguish. Large caliber fire hit the vehicles. Grenades and pistol flares howled over our heads. Finally, after much shouting and confusion, the Fascists began to fire their heavy weapons.... After very intense fighting we retreated slowly towards Moscow, leaving behind us a large number of enemy dead and ruined vehicles . . .[41]

The Fourth Panzer Army, experiencing great difficulty with the hard-fighting Russian rearguard units, slogged forward foot by foot, and on 12 October, it reported that advance units had reached Kaluga and Maloyaroslavets. From the latter city a paved highway led through Naro-Fominsk to the Soviet capital. During the night of 12–13 October, German tanks slipped through Naro-Fominsk, but the destroyed bridges across the Moscow River and desperate resistance by Russian cavalrymen halted their advance. They were within forty miles of Moscow.

On the southern sector of the front, Guderian's advance was slower. An attempt to seize Tula failed with considerable losses in men and tanks. Other units in Guderian's Second Panzer Army succeeded, however, in reaching Stalinogorsk and Venev, two smaller towns northeast of Tula. This movement indicated that Tula could be probably bypassed and a pocket formed around that city, trapping the defenders.

In Germany, radio stations interrupted their normal programs several times during the course of the day to announce: "We expect an important special bulletin within a short time. Please stand by."[42] In Berlin, Hamburg, Munich, and a dozen other German cities, evening newspapers headlined the impending fall of Moscow. The Nazi Party's official newspaper, *Der Völkische Beobachter,* was the most dramatic of all. In huge, red, glaring headlines it announced: "The Great Hour Has Come! The Eastern Campaign Has Ended!"[43]

Throughout the cities, towns, and villages of Germany, rumors spread like wildfire among the populace. "Moscow has fallen!" "Stalin has asked for an armistice!" "Peace! Peace!"[44] In Berlin, a butcher welcomed all comers into his store and passed out free gifts of prized sausages in celebration of the great victory. In Nürnberg, a shopowner advised a housewife, who wished to purchase a fancy postcard to send to her soldier-husband "somewhere on the Eastern front," to go home and await the good news that her husband would soon be returning home.[45]

And in Moscow there was panic. Hundreds of thousands of Muscovites, mainly old men, women, and children, began to evacuate the city. Still more hundreds of thousands were ordered to form emergency volunteer units for the city's defense. For a while the police and law enforcement agencies of the city of Moscow lost control, and there was considerable looting and pillaging of deserted shops and stores. Violators who were caught were executed on the spot.[46]

On 12 October, Stalin called an urgent meeting of the Central Committee of the Communist Party. It was decided to evacuate the gargantuan apparatus of the Soviet Russian national government to Kuibyshev, a city in the Ural Mountains about 500 miles southeast of Moscow. It was also decided to relieve Marshal Timoshenko from command of the Western Front and to appoint in his place General of the Army G. K. Zhukov as commander of all Russian forces defending Moscow. Zhukov's deputy commander was General V. D. Sokolovsky.[47]

Bock's air pilots made numerous flights over the city. They could see smoke from hundreds of small fires in or near the government buildings, as Russian officials burned documents, archives, and paraphernalia that could not be immediately evacuated.[48]

A Russian historian has described the situation candidly: The battles on the approaches to Moscow became ever more intense. . . . On the night of 12–13 October, Secretary A. S. Shcherbakov of the Moscow City Soviet addressed a meeting of the Soviet. He stated that the capital was in grave danger and that during the past few days the military situation had deteriorated badly. "An extremely bitter fight has been raging day and night," stated Comrade Shcherbakov. "Our forces are conducting themselves in the most heroic manner. The enemy is incurring severe losses. Hundreds of his tanks and planes are being destroyed. His loss of lives exceeds that of any other conflict in history. Despite this, however, our heroic men are being forced back. Most of our cities and installations on the western approaches to our capital are in Fascist hands. The battle is now developing on the very borders of the Moscow District. Let us not close our eyes, Comrades, to the fact that Moscow is in imminent danger." Shcherbakov reminded his listeners that the Bolsheviks had always faced dangerous situations with reality. He called upon all Communists and workers of the beloved capital to expend their utmost efforts to repel the enemy....

On the morning of 13 October the entire city was placed in a state of emergency.... The evacuation of industrial installations, governmental agencies, ministries, and institutions was accelerated.... Many art works and items of historical value were carried away or secured.... In these critical days the strength and courage of the Soviet people were put to the supreme test.... Workers reported to their local party leaders or war commissars and demanded to be sent to the front. Men and women, even children, worked mightily to bolster the city's fortifications....

There were isolated incidents of disorder and confusion among the population.... Some workers deserted their places of duty and attempted to flee the city.... There were traitors who took advantage of the critical situation to plunder and steal socialist property and to undermine the power of the Soviet state. These predators and traitors were strongly resisted by the general population....."[49]

Throughout the period, Bock was in frequent communication with Brauchitsch. Optimistically, Brauchitsch suggested that in view of the heavy fortifications that air units reported were being thrown up in Moscow proper, it might be less costly in manpower if Bock encircled the city on a radius of about twenty miles from its center. Bock agreed. Brauchitsch wanted to know the approximate time in which the city could be termed safe and secure, as there were indications from Armed Forces High Command that Hitler himself wished to make a triumphant entry into Moscow, along with the main body of Bock's forces. Bock replied that Hitler would be informed in good time.[50]

Two events now occurred that had ominous significance. The first was that all along the front, Russian resistance suddenly stiffened. To the north, several divisions of the Ninth Army, ordered to capture Kalinin and exploit the breakthrough that had been made earlier by the Third Panzer Army, ran head-on into fresh Russian units. The Germans were forced to fall back from Kalinin with considerable losses. A counterattack west of Kalinin managed to stabilize the situation. What surprised and puzzled the German commanders, however, was that men of Mongol origin were among the Russian prisoners that had been captured in the bitter fighting. They wore warm, quilted uniforms, and, upon interrogation, German intelligence officers discovered that they could not speak Russian.[51]

The same thing happened in the Fourth Army's sector due west of Moscow, when some of Kluge's divisions attacked Svenigorod, less than thirty miles from the Soviet capital. Farther to the south, Russian units, fresh and spirited, attacked Guderian's weary tankmen and drove them out of Stalinogorsk and Venev. Again German local counterattacks restored the situation, but the two Russian towns remained, for the time being, in Russian hands. During the Russian assault, German commanders in the area received an even greater shock than their hard-fighting colleagues to the north. For the first time in the German-Russian war, the Russians brought out their new tank, the fearsome T-34. Guderian's tank and anti-tank crews looked on in utter astonishment as the wide-tracked, low-slung T-34 tank careened over the deep mud and slush that had bogged down the German panzers, with their narrower tracks and smaller bogie wheels. The Germans were even more astonished when shells from their 75-millimeter tank guns ricocheted off the Russian tanks.

Guderian sent an immediate report to Army Group Center, in which he stated that the appearance of the Russian T-34 tanks on the battlefront had established tactical superiority over the more lightly equipped German armored forces. He demanded that a commission of army ordnance and armor experts be sent to his sector for the dual purpose of investigating this unpleasant development and of designing immediately a German tank that would at least have parity with the Russian tank.[52]

The second significant occurrence was a turn in the weather. It suddenly became worse. Rain, sleet, and snow fell continuously from Lake Onega, far to the north, to the southern Ukraine. Since the temperature was not cold enough to freeze the ground solidly, the Russian terrain became a bottomless sea of mud. It clung like molten lead to men, animals, and machines. Field Marshal von Bock's military machine floundered hopelessly in the morass. It finally came to a complete halt.

The Russians took advantage of the bad weather and exploded huge craters and every bridge along the paved highways leading to Moscow. With this action Bock lost his chance to capture Moscow in mid-October.

Regarding these unfavorable developments, Bock remained outwardly phlegmatic. He talked to all of his senior commanders—at least those whom he could contact by telephone and radio—and was told without exception that forward movement by any unit was, for the moment, impossible. He reported to Army High Command that Army Group Center was stuck in the Russian mud. And he noted in his diary that he was very concerned for the future of the operation and for the morale of the officers and men in Army Group Center. "All of them are asking themselves: what is going to happen to us now?" Bock wrote.[53]

In Berlin, the edition of *Der Völkische Beobachter* for 16 October carried the following headline: "E-boats [fast patrol boats] Sink Six Freighters in North Sea!" There was no reference whatsoever to the bitter campaign raging on the approaches to Moscow.[54]

As if to compensate for the frustration of failure, Bock returned his attention to the Bryansk and Vyasma pockets, which had been sealed off for several days and were being relentlessly narrowed down by infantry and security units. By 18 October the pockets were completely liquidated. On 19 October, Bock issued an order of the day.

SOLDIERS OF ARMY GROUP CENTER!

The battles of Vyasma and Bryansk are now concluded!
They have resulted in a complete collapse of the Russian front! In these great battles of encirclement against a numerically superior enemy you have destroyed:

8 armies, consisting of 73 rifle and cavalry divisions.

You have captured:

673,098 prisoners.	4,378 heavy artillery pieces.
1,277 tanks.	1,009 anti-tank and anti-aircraft guns.
187 aircraft.	

Incalculable amounts of small arms, munitions, vehicles of every description, and war supplies!

In this most difficult battle you have performed the greatest feat of arms in history! Again you have acquitted yourselves with honor and glory befitting German soldiers!

To all commanders and troops of Army Group Center, both on and behind the front, I congratulate you on the occasion of this historic success, and I express to you sincerest appreciation and highest recognition!

> Bock
> *Field Marshal*[55]

On the next day, 20 October, Bock left his headquarters in a heavy, tracked command car, which made its way along the cratered highway toward Vyasma. He wanted to see for himself the extent of the difficulty his units were having. Bock noted:

It is truly incredible. Even the supposedly first-class roads are practically impassable. Repairing them and the bridges that the Russians have blown up is so hindered by mud that the task is almost impossible. Even if a single supply truck gets through the men consider that an achievement. . . . I am concerned that the hundreds of thousands of prisoners moving west of Vyasma in the direction of Smolensk are poorly guarded. . . . It is a gruesome sight. Totally starved and half-dead, these unfortunate men slog along, barely able to move one foot after the other. They beg for a scrap of food. Countless dead lie along the road. . . . I discuss this awful situation with my commanders, but it is impossible to help these men. . . . We must find a way, however, to guard them more closely and get them into prisoner of war camps expeditiously, else thousands will escape and become partisans behind our front. . . .[56]

A few days later a group of German war correspondents managed to make their way to the Bryansk battlefield. One wrote:

It was not necessary to search far for signs of the great battle. They were all around. We climbed through the mud to some high ground, overlooking a birch forest. The entire area was covered with the Bolsheviks' wrecked vehicles. Our bombers and tanks and artillery had hit with devastating effect among the retreating columns, destroying men, animals, and equipment alike. Everywhere lay broken rifles, cartridge belts by the thousands, crushed steel helmets, tattered uniforms, shells of all calibers, shell-casings, tanks with turrets blown off, and demolished guns. They lay in the underbrush, in the fields, in the bunkers and foxholes, where our brave men had rooted out the Bolsheviks, man by man. Strange, little gray-green boxes were scattered about by the hundreds. We kicked them with our muddy boots, but we knew that they were the frightful wooden mines, now defused, that the Bolsheviks used. . . . It was a picture of chaos and the deadly ferocity of modern battle. It all assumed an even more abominable aspect in the cold, hostile, dreary October morning.[57]

In terms of masses of men, machines, and equipment involved, and especially of the stupendous Russian losses, the dual battles of Vyasma-Bryansk compare with the greatest in military history. For Bock and Army Group Center, they represented an overwhelming tactical success. Bock was sincere when he proclaimed in his order of the day that the battles had resulted in a collapse of the Russian front. The Russians, in his professional estimation, could not possibly recover from the loss of almost 700,000 prisoners alone, not counting the dead and wounded, and not counting their previous losses in manpower, territory, and industrial installations.

Bock's losses had also been heavy, and they were losses that he could ill afford. The Vyasma-Bryansk battlefields were littered with crude, makeshift crosses over the graves of German dead. But Bock's greatest loss of all was time. And his loss had been the Russians' gain. Although the military situation was, for the Russians, still extremely critical, and although they probably expected Moscow to fall, the city still stood, and Bock's advance forces still remained bogged in the mud, a tantalizingly scant forty miles from the Soviet Russian capital.

In apparent indemnification for the grand announcement of the fall of Moscow which never came, the German radio broadcast in dramatic statements the victories at Vyasma and Bryansk, repeating the Armed Forces High Command bulletin many times during the next few days.[58]

On the front before Moscow, Bock searched for ways and means to continue the attack. Some of his units were able to move forward only with the greatest difficulty; others reported that movement was impossible. On 21 October, units of Strauss's Ninth Army, slogging forward with dogged tenacity, captured Kalinin. In the south, Guderian's XLIII Panzer Corps managed to cross the flooding Oka River and to take Serpukhov and Kashira. Other units under Guderian's command advanced to within two miles of Tula, but just when it appeared that this important city would fall, the Russians counterattacked savagely and drove them back. In the central sectors, units of Kluge's Fourth Army straddled the Moscow River, which, like all rivers and tributaries in the area, was overrunning its banks, and advanced slowly yard by yard. Here, too, all movement was difficult. Kluge's men hoped to use the Moscow River as flank security, and although vanguards of the 4th Panzer Division actually approached within sight of Moscow's spires, they were forced to retreat as darkness fell, under threat of being cut off by Russians who had attacked behind them.[59]

Reports reaching Bock's headquarters told of incredible feats by his exhausted men as they inched forward in the mud. In some cases, they used horses in teams of up to thirty-six to tow their heavy guns and tanks which had sunk into the morass. As one desperate measure, Bock commanded all motorized units in Army Group Center that were bogged down behind the front to dismount, abandon their vehicles, and move ahead on foot, to assist the infantry and artillery units that were closer to their prize—Moscow. "All of these units are of no use behind the front; at least, they can try to make headway in this manner," he surmised.[60]

With any type of movement, either directly at the fighting front or in the rear areas, almost an impossibility, supplies dwindled rapidly. Emergency supplies of food and fuel had long since been used up in many units. Hundreds of Bock's lower commanders placed their battalions and companies on emergency rations, which often consisted of one loaf of bread and a small can of beef for every ten men. In most cases, however, even this scanty amount was not forthcoming. One result was that the morale and confidence of Bock's Army Group Center began to decline seriously.

The situation caused Bock great concern. While he had no compunction about demanding superhuman efforts of his officers and men, he knew well that a decline of morale in such adverse conditions would endanger the entire military operation. Bock held urgent conferences with the supply officers of his staff. He was told that the supplies that were now reaching the front-line troops had dwindled in past days to less than twenty-five percent of minimum daily requirements. The most critical shortage was food.

On 22 October, Bock left his headquarters and, escorted by a column of heavily armed vehicles, went forward to visit his units. Near the town of Istra, about thirty miles west of Moscow, he talked to the commander and men of the 258th Infantry Division. The physically exhausted soldiers did their best to make a good impression for their field marshal, but a far less practiced eye than Bock's could see that the men were almost at the end of human endurance. The endless, strenuous hours of struggling in the mud and fighting off the tenacious Russians were exacting a frightful toll.

Bock spoke encouragingly to individual soldiers, as he and his entourage moved laboriously over the muddy terrain from one infantry position to another. He noted that many men appeared to be ill with severe colds and respiratory ailments. But he also noted that many soldiers were resorting to ingenious methods to compensate for or to supplement their inadequate supplies, especially of clothing and food. To protect themselves against the incessant, cold rains, the soldiers had erected camouflaged shelters and lean-tos of every description. Since the entire division had been bogged down in the Istra area for more than two weeks, being totally unable to advance, many soldiers had also constructed underground bunkers as protection against the bad weather and sporadic Russian fire. The bunkers were so constructed that they were practically dry and the soldiers who inhabited them were fairly comfortable. In one such bunker that Bock visited, the soldiers offered to share with him a succulent roast duck, which an hour before had been the sole live occupant of an abandoned Russian farm.

Inwardly, Bock felt pity for his thousands of uncomfortable men. Outwardly, he maintained his usual cold, lofty demeanor, and in every instance he exhorted the soldiers and their commanders to put forth a supreme effort to attain the final goal.[61]

Upon returning to his headquarters, Bock pored over war maps and reports, conferred with his commanders and staff officers, debated and discussed operational matters with higher headquarters, and received official visitors. During the last days of October, Dr. Wilhelm Todt, Minister of Armaments in the Third Reich, lunched with von Bock. On the same day, the Swiss military attaché, Colonel Reinhard Bircher, came and stayed for dinner. On 24 October, General Rinaldo Muñoz-Grandes, commander of the Spanish "Blue Division" which was fighting alongside the Germans in Russia, spent an hour with Bock. On 25 October, *Reichsführer-SS* Heinrich Himmler paid a call on von Bock and conferred with him for several hours.[62]

On the next day, Army High Command notified Bock that the Italian Premier, Benito Mussolini, might possibly fly to Smolensk in the very near future. Mussolini's visit, however, did not materialize.

Two of Bock's senior commanders, Hoepner and von Weichs, also made personal calls. Both expressed concern, as Bock did, over the untenable position in which their armies found themselves because of the adverse weather and the time being given to the Russians to recover. But neither could offer to Bock's satisfaction any constructive suggestions for extricating themselves from the perilous situation. Hoepner hinted broadly at the feasibility of withdrawing to a "winter line of defense," anchored on Kholm-Smolensk-Roslavl. Bock dismissed Hoepner's hint as completely impractical.[63]

On 26 October, the weather improved slightly. The snow ceased, and in some areas of Army Group Center's expansive front the sun shone briefly. But the ground remained a morass of mud and slush. Again Guderian's forces made a determined attempt to seize Tula, and again they were repelled with heavy losses. The Russians apparently were as determined to hold Tula as Moscow.

On 27 October, Bock left his headquarters and went to the Smolensk railroad station. The 1st Cavalry Division, one of the older units in the German Army, was being transferred back to Germany to be inactivated and reorganized into a panzer division. As a younger general, Bock had commanded the 1st Cavalry Division some fifteen years earlier. In honor of their former commander, now the field marshal, the men of the 1st Cavalry Division, some of whom were veterans of two world wars, held a review parade before boarding the train for home. Perhaps von Bock remembered the peace and prosperity of earlier years in his beloved Prussia, when he had led the old cavalry soldiers. Or, perhaps he was wavering ever so slightly under the tremendous pressure of conducting the Russian campaign. At any rate the usually aloof, arrogant, impersonal von Bock displayed deep emotion as he stood on the platform near the Smolensk railroad station, watching the traditional "pass in review" ceremony to the strains of the *"Fehrbelliner Reitermarsch."*

"Those old horsemen will never be forgotten," he noted. "It is a sad symbol of the times that cavalrymen are no longer needed in this war."[64]

During the next days the weather remained relatively mild, and Bock was encouraged to consider a resumption of the general offensive. He realized that his forces had been badly hurt during the past month, both by the bad weather and by the Russians' stubborn, tenacious resistance. Combat casualties in Army Group Center now exceeded 200,000.[65] This was a high figure, but it was still low in comparison to the astronomical casualty rates of the First World War. However, the number of reported illnesses had risen alarmingly during past weeks since the onset of bad weather. Thousand's of Bock's men, inadequately clothed and exposed continuously to the inclement weather, had contracted pneumonia, influenza, typhus, and that dreaded disease that has always plagued soldiers who must fight in wet, cold climates—trenchfoot. When the sick and incapacitated were included in Bock's losses, the number approached 300,000. In many cases, manpower strength in battalions and companies had been reduced by forty percent. Moreover, Army High Command had informed Bock that the number of available replacements could not redress the losses.[66]

In addition, to resume a general attack, the supply situation would have to be vastly improved. The serious, ever-present supply problem weighed as heavily upon Bock as the manpower losses. Not only armaments, munitions, equipment, and vehicles, but also the vital necessities for daily subsistence were grossly inadequate. There were two major methods of supplying Bock's forces in Russia—by railroad and by vehicle. Both methods were proving insufficient for the gigantic task. German trucks, with their two-wheeled drive, simply could not negotiate the muddy, often undefined trails that passed for roads in most of Russia. Mechanical breakdowns were almost too numerous to count. A similar situation prevailed with railway equipment. Russian railroads used a wider gauge track than the German. This meant that German supply trains had to be trans-loaded onto Russian trains, or the tracks had to be re-laid to narrower German gauge. In either case, it was a preponderous task, and there never seemed to be enough men to perform it.

In contrast to the irretrievable losses in manpower, Bock had been repeatedly assured, as a result of his complaints, that vast stocks of supplies, including winter clothing, were piled up in warehouses and at railway sidings in Warsaw, Brest-Litovsk, and intermediate sites. The major problem, therefore, was not inadequate supplies but lack of means to transport them to the proper locations, that is, to the troops on the fighting front. Bock had urged his rear area commander, Schenckendorff, to rectify this situation as soon as possible.[67]

Above all, Bock reasoned that if his forces had been badly bruised in the recent fighting, the Russians were in a far worse condition. He therefore decided to order a resumption of the general offensive on 1 November. His intention was to enter Moscow on 7 November.

But von Bock was again to be thwarted. On 29 October, when he informed Army High Command of his plans, a reply came back ordering Army Group Center to cease all forward movement now and in the near future. Bock called Army High Command to protest. He talked to Brigadier General Adolf Heusinger, who was representing Halder while the latter recovered from a horseback riding accident. Heusinger rightly claimed that he was in no position to reverse the order or to change it in any form. He tried to placate Bock by assuring him the matter would be referred to his chief, Halder, at the earliest possible time. Bock rang off with the caustic remark that the Army Group Center situation and daily reports apparently merited no consideration at Army High Command. There is no record that Bock attempted to consult the officer who perhaps could have given authoritative attention to his dilemma, Army Commander-in-Chief Brauchitsch. If he did in fact contact Brauchitsch, the order remained unchanged for the time being; if he did not, the reason why remains a mystery.[68]

This incident did not end Bock's troubles with Army High Command. In fact, the troubles increased. Early on the next morning came still another directive from Army High Command. The directive ordered Guderian's Second Panzer Army to make a turning movement to its right and to attack Voronezh, a Ukrainian city on the Don River, almost 400 miles southeast of Moscow. The reasoning for such a move, stated Army High Command, was to eliminate the perennial threat to Guderian's right flank and to establish more stable communications between Army Group Center and South.

Bock wondered how Army High Command thought it possible to extract a huge tank army from the mud and send it off in a southerly direction, when the entire focus of the attack was aimed at Moscow. He had regained some of his composure after the sharply worded conversation with Heusinger. In the remote event that Army High Command's order had slight merit, he contacted Guderian to learn what opinions the latter might have. Guderian refused even to consider the matter. "A practical impossibility!" Guderian stormed. "There are no highways at all leading from here to Voronezh. Besides my units are concentrating for an attack on Tula, and to attempt to turn them around would be the height of folly!"[69]

Bock then called Army High Command. This time he talked to Brauchitsch and stated with finality that the order could not be executed. Brauchitsch replied, somewhat coldly, that due cognizance would be taken of Bock's statements. Some hours later an order rescinding the Voronezh attack reached Army Group Center.

The situation became more and more critical for Army Group Center, and an irreparable gap seemed to be developing in its relations with Army High Command. Not only this, but Bock's own position seemed to become ever more precarious. The next event was to bear this out.

During the afternoon of 29 October, Field Marshal Keitel, Chief of Staff of Armed Forces High Command and the military man who was closest to Hitler, called directly to Bock's headquarters. Keitel talked not to Bock but to Greiffenberg, Army Group Center's Chief of Staff. He stated that Field Marshal von Kluge must report to Hitler's headquarters in East Prussia at once, and that Hitler's private plane would arrive that same afternoon to fetch Kluge. When Bock was informed of this development he was indignant. "This is a sad state of affairs," he lamented. "I am not to represent Army Group Center in its critical time."[70]

Late in the afternoon Hitler's plane landed at Smolensk with Hitler's personal adjutant, Schmundt, aboard. Schmundt did not talk to Bock either, but waited at planeside until Kluge arrived after a hasty flight from Fourth Army's headquarters.

After an overnight stay at Hitler's headquarters Kluge returned to Smolensk and called on Bock, perhaps in deference to his superior officer. Kluge stated that Hitler appeared to have a good grasp of the conditions in Army Group Center, especially those facing Fourth Army. "Hitler does not, however, permit himself to believe the written reports from Army Group Center with regard to manpower shortages, supply difficulties, impassable roads, and the like," Kluge stated. "He is very disturbed that Moscow has not yet fallen and considers it impossible that we could not have foreseen all of the contingencies."[71]

Bock was skeptical and sarcastic. "That is hardly to be

wondered at," he replied. "Naturally, Hitler will not be convinced that it was his own strategic error last August that has gotten us into this mess. Now we are stuck in the mud up to our knees and Moscow may as well be 400 miles away, for we are unable to extricate ourselves and advance the remaining short distance!"[72]

On the night of 30 October, the Russian weather struck again with full fury. A blizzard raged over the entire area of the front, and again Army Group Center's soldiers and vehicles bogged down in the snow and mud. Reluctantly, Bock postponed the general attack. "Our only alternative now is to wait and hope for the ground to freeze hard. Still the situation is very doubtful."[73] Bock stood at the window of his offices, stared for a long time at the wintry weather, and thought of the misery that his hundreds of thousands of soldiers were enduring. "I wonder how they can survive," he mused. "Our strength will now become even more depleted."[74]

Bock returned to his desk, laden with piles of papers and reports. A particular document caught his eye. It was a general situation report on the German Eleventh Army's conquest of the Russian Crimea. The report noted that the sun was shining in the Crimea, the temperature in the fifties. Bock walked back to the window and stared again at the raging winter storm. He pictured the pleasant sunshine and the dry ground far away on the great Russian steppe, over a thousand miles to the south. For the second time in a few days, Bock became sentimental. He even permitted himself a moment of self-pity. "I envy them down there," he thought. "They are making progress and are knocking the wind out of the Russians. Here we cannot do that. We are bogged down almost hopelessly in the mud and snow."[75]

The weather worsened. On 2 November, Bock received a delayed telegram from Propaganda Minister Dr. Josef Goebbels. The telegram stated that Goebbels had attempted to reach Bock's headquarters but had been forced to turn back a short distance east of Minsk. Neither plane nor automobile could negotiate the mired roads and cyclonic winds. The telegram was signed personally by Goebbels. It stated that Goebbels and his entourage had attempted unsuccessfully to reach Smolensk at the behest of Hitler, and it suggested that perhaps in view of adverse developments Field Marshal von Bock might wish to submit a letter of resignation to the Führer. In reward for his long years of patriotic service to the German Reich, the telegram read, the city of Smolensk would bear Bock's name after final victory over the Bolsheviks. It would be called "Bockburg."

Coldly furious, Bock replied that, as a rule, German officers did not and should not accept presents of this kind, and he himself had no intention of doing so. However, Bock concluded, if it were the Führer's wish he "would be happy to submit his resignation."[76]

Bock received no answer to his message to Dr. Goebbels.

On 5 November, the temperature dropped to minus twenty degrees Fahrenheit. The snow ceased, but the skies remained overcast. The ground froze to a depth of several inches all along the front. "This makes movement a bit easier," Bock noted.[77]

But now the cold weather only added to the miseries of Bock's soldiers. Most of them still had no winter coats; many men were severely frostbitten and required evacuation. Some of the more ingenious stuffed papers, rags, or other such materials inside their uniforms and boots as meager protection against the cold. The engines in their tanks and trucks refused to start. The soldiers ate their hard bread and their potato soup, which froze in minutes, and hoped for better days to come.

Despite their handicaps, however, some of Bock's forces, especially on the southern flank, made progress. The Second Army managed to secure the highway between Orel and Kursk, accomplishing to a lesser degree the objective that higher headquarters had in mind when it had directed an attack toward Voronezh a week earlier. Guderian reported that he intended to attack Tula once again but was being harassed by Russian attacks from the direction of Yefremov. Bock flew in subzero weather to Guderian's headquarters at Orel to confer with him. Neither man could find any basis for optimism. In his frank manner, Guderian told his commander that the chance to deliver a final, knockout blow to the Russians was fast disappearing.[78]

Back at his headquarters, Bock's attention was momentarily diverted by an event that had international overtones. The 638th Infantry Regiment, an organization of French volunteer soldiers, had arrived for assignment to the combat forces of Army Group Center. The regiment had been expected since shortly after the beginning of the Russian campaign. It was several months late. Marshal Henri Petain, the Premier of the French Vichy government, had specifically requested that a French liaison officer remain with Army Group Center, and Hitler's government had acceded to the request. Bock received the French officer cordially and advised him that the regiment would be assigned to the 7th Infantry Division. He stated that the divisional commander, Major General Fritz von Rappard, would be instructed to assist the French soldiers in every way possible. Bock noted that the French soldiers were wearing German Army uniforms. After the liaison officer departed he directed that the divisional commander be instructed to handle the German-uniformed French soldiers with caution, to see to it that they did not lose morale and discipline in the adverse circumstances, because this would be harmful to his own men. About a week later Bock noted in a report that the French regiment had been withdrawn from the fighting front.[79]

During the next days the temperature continued to fall until it stood at thirty degrees below zero. Bock noted that the rivers and streams along the front froze to sufficient thickness to support vehicular traffic. He reflected that at least his overworked engineers would get a respite from repairing numerous destroyed bridges. But he also noted a serious rise in the number of casualties due to frostbite and fatigue. Bock's Army Group Center was tiring.

On 8 November, Russian troops, equipped with snow skis and winter uniforms, suddenly attacked Kalinin, the base for the northern prong of Bock's attack. Determined to hold the city rather than to be driven out in the merciless winter weather, the Germans fought viciously to repel the Russians. A Red Army officer who was captured in the fighting, identified himself upon being questioned as a member of the Sixty-First Army. Ninth Army sent the interrogation report to Bock's headquarters with the notation that this was a new Red Army organization on the front, which a few weeks earlier had been stationed in eastern Siberia.[80]

On 10 November, a detailed, highly classified study from Army High Command arrived at Bock's headquarters. As far as Bock could ascertain, the study had been prepared without the knowledge of Hitler or any high members of his military staff. The study pertained to the utilization of Russian prisoners of war in "special units" on the Russian front. It noted that the German Army held in excess of 3,500,000 Russian prisoners and that many of these men had indicated a willingness to fight against the Stalinist regime. The report mentioned no Russian names but inferred that several very high Russian officers who were now prisoners of war, including an army commander captured at Vyasma, could, if properly utilized, become assets to the German war effort in Russia, since German manpower was reaching a critical shortage. The report asked Bock for his comments.

Even in the midst of the greatest operational difficulties and the prospect of failure looming before him, von Bock remained a conservative, unbending militarist. He simply could not bring himself favorably to consider the idea of Russians and Germans fighting for the same cause. He therefore replied:

My opinion is that the use of special units composed of Russian prisoners is an infraction on the duties and rights of the German Army . . . . As long as it is able to do so, the Army has the responsibility to observe the rules of warfare with regard to the treatment of prisoners. Authority for the handling of prisoners of war is delegated to the camp commanders, and military police are given the right to decide what prisoner is to be assigned to a special unit and what prisoner is not. . . . If, however, it is decided to organize special units of prisoners, I strongly recommend that they be held in the rear areas. Even then this should be done only after considering the most important political necessities. Since these are not within the realm of a military commander, I recommend, in the event the special units are organized, that they be kept *outside* the administration of my army group. . . .

Bock

Field Marshal[81]

Bock heard no more of the proposal during the remainder of the campaign.

On 10 November, Bock learned that Field Marshal von Brauchitsch had suffered a serious heart attack. Bock telegraphed him a message of sympathy and best wishes for recovery.

Meanwhile, the crisis became more and more serious. The temperature sank to forty degrees below zero. It required no military genius to realize that Army Group Center was in danger of annihilation if it remained stationary before the gates of Moscow in the arctic weather. There were two alternatives: withdraw or attack. Again Bock ruled out any consideration of withdrawing his forces and issued preparatory orders for an attack to begin on 17 November. During the next days Bock hoped that the supply situation would somehow improve. Reserve stocks of supplies of all categories had practically disappeared. Although losses of vehicles were mounting steadily, unit commanders had been forced to order the remaining vehicles to be limited to a few gallons of fuel for each vehicle. Similarly, heavy artillery units were rationed to eight or ten shells per day, an intolerably insufficient amount to support a renewed attack. Nevertheless, Bock was determined to attack. He commanded every supply agency in Army Group Center to exert the utmost effort to improve the supply situation and instructed his chief of staff to prepare the appropriate attack order. Greiffenberg was not in accord with a continuation of the attack, but he was a loyal, capable officer and not inclined to oppose Bock. He prepared the order and then contacted Halder, who had returned to duty, to inform him of Bock's decision.

Greiffenberg's communication with Halder, however, had unpleasant results. Halder stated flatly that in his opinion the timing of Army Group Center's proposed new attack was in error; and furthermore, it would be helpful if Army Group Center remained in closer communication with Army High Command.[82]

Upon hearing this, Bock called Halder:

The objective that Army High Command has assigned to Army Group Center can no longer be attained, because of diminishing troop strength and a critical shortage of supplies. ... In other words, it is no longer possible to encircle Moscow. Accordingly, I have set as long-range objectives the attainment of a line running through Sagorsk and Dmitrov in the north and Orekhov-Suyevo in the south. Even this is a farfetched goal, and I shall be very happy if we can attain it. Our intermediate goal is to reach the Moscow-Volga Canal in the north and the confluence of the Moscow-Oka Rivers in the south, or in the vicinity of Kolomna. For the purpose of attaining these objectives I propose to attack on the date previously stated (17 November). . . . Even then, I am not sure that we can reach these targets, and we may have to settle for shorter-range objectives. . . . The greatest problem is to obtain supplies. . . . The Quartermaster General, with whom I have spoken recently, has promised to furnish at least sufficient munitions for the attack. . . . Most importantly, I want it understood that it is no longer possible to execute a classical operation here. The time has passed for that, or any other large-scale deployment of troops. . . . Also, I cannot suggest how long we will be able to sustain an attack of any proportions. There is a serious decline in morale and confidence among the troops. Losses are very high. The weather conditions are indescribable, and if we get more snow it will bring an end to any movement at all. . . .[83]

Halder's reply was to suggest an urgent conference of all commanders on the Eastern Front, to be held at a place that was relatively central and accessible to all who would attend. Bock and Halder agreed that the best place was Orsha, a sizable town on the Dnieper about sixty miles west of Smolensk. The time of the conference would be on the next day, 12 November. A German historian has captured the scene:

On 12 November the thermometer stood at about thirty-five degrees below zero. . . . It was a lively day for the airfield at Orsha. Halder's plane arrived from Rastenburg, East Prussia, and the planes of the army group and army commanders arrived one after another. . . . Halder had summoned them to a conference. The subject of the conference was: what was to be done? Should the divisions dig in, take up winter quarters, and wait for spring? Or should the offensive—mainly against

Moscow—be continued in spite of the weather? The conference at Orsha is of particular significance in the history of the war. It probably provides the answer to a question argued to this day: who was ultimately responsible for the resumption of the ill-fated winter offensive?

Bock argued for a continuation of the offensive as a military and psychological necessity. . . . In the Führer's headquarters it was believed that the Russians were at the end of their tether and that one last effort would defeat them completely. Bock did not share this optimism; he knew the condition of his troops and realized that only a short span of time was left. . . . But Bock regarded the offensive as a better alternative than spending a desolate winter in the field. . . . There was the danger that they might not succeed, but this was no worse than lying on open ground in the snow and cold only thirty miles from the tempting objectives. . . .[84]

And so, it was decided to continue the offensive. Was it still possible to capture Moscow? Bock thought so; Halder thought so; Guderian thought there was a slight chance; Kluge was noncommittal. Certainly Hitler, following the progress of Army Group Center on his great war map in East Prussia, thought so.

A large number of Bock's more stout-hearted soldiers thought that they still could get into Moscow, too. But then only the stout of heart had managed to survive thus far the terrible ordeal of battle, the subzero weather, and the sickness. Now, even some of these men succumbed. Their physical strength failed, and many thousands simply lay down on the snowy ground to freeze to death.

After the Orsha conference, Bock returned to his headquarters and busied himself with getting the attack started. He issued a terse order of the day, in which he exhorted the forces of Army Group Center to make a final effort to defeat the enemy and reach the objective. He stated to his exhausted men that reserves were being sent forward to assist them, and although he realized the hardships they were enduring, the German soldier was still superior to the Russian and therefore victory would ultimately come.[85]

Bock experienced great difficulty in having his orders executed. The Second and Ninth Infantry Armies made some painful progress, but the panzer armies, especially Guderian's and Kluge's Fourth Army were unable or unwilling to attack on 17 November. Bock turned his attention, first, to Guderian, literally bombarding him with telegraphed instructions. Guderian replied that he was confronted with fresh enemy forces and that he was doing the best that he could. "This is not France in May, you know!" he berated Bock, referring to the more pleasant blitzkrieg days of 1940.[86] Nevertheless, Guderian's tanks struck north and east of Tula, covering about three miles at the end of the first day of the attack.

Next Bock turned to Kluge, who had also postponed his attack. In reply to Bock's demand for clarification of his plans, Kluge sardonically asked: "Where are the reserves that you mentioned?"[87] Bock's retort to this was, in effect, "Stop procrastinating and proceed with the attack!"[88] It was apparent that tempers were becoming as short as time. To assuage von Kluge, as well as to attempt to give weight to the attack, Bock ordered the commitment of the last combat reserves, which consisted of three infantry divisions. The only reserve forces that were now left to Army Group Center were a security division and several police battalions. But Bock's divisions were becoming ineffective faster than he could possibly replace them. The losses in several were so heavy that they had to be inactivated. In all others, companies that had started Operation *Typhoon* with 150 men were reporting only thirty or forty men who were still on their feet; regiments with an original strength of 2500 men could often count less than 400. Losses of officers were particularly heavy, and in many instances lieutenants were commanding battalions, even regiments.

On 20 November, Bock ordered his special train to be moved up to the most advanced point of the fighting front, so that he could assume personal direction of this final attempt to take Moscow. The train stopped at the Istra railroad station, about thirty miles west of Moscow. From there Bock made his tortuous way farther forward in one of Hoepner's tanks to an artillery command post located about ten miles from the center of the city. The freezing winds blew with hurricane force, and the swirling snow and ice decreased visibility. Yet von Bock was sufficiently close to the Soviet capital to see with his field glasses the outlines of the city. That was as close as Bock himself ever got to Moscow.

Upon his return to his special train, a long telegram was awaiting Bock from Hitler. The telegram instructed Bock to desist from mounting frontal attacks and to concentrate on an encirclement of the city from the north and south. Since the northern prong showed promise of better success, Hitler stated, Bock should support it by committing more troops to Hoepner's and Reinhardt's tank armies.

"Where will I get the troops?" Bock wondered.[89]

He drafted a reply for transmission to Hitler, in which he stated that Army Group Center had no more troops left to conduct a concerted movement of encirclement. Moreover, supplies were practically nonexistent. In fact, there was a strong possibility that Army Group Center would not be able to accomplish its mission. Bock concluded the report to Hitler with the statement that at least thirty-four new Russian divisions had been identified on the front. As far as he could ascertain, all of these fresh Russian troops had not as yet been thrown into the fight. When that happened, the fate of Army Group Center would hang in the balance.[90]

In spite of the bitter cold, the deep snow, and the lack of

supplies, the exhausted soldiers of Army Group Center made a little progress. After several days of the most desperate efforts, the 7th Panzer Division, Third Panzer Army, crossed the frozen Moscow-Volga Canal and moved along its eastern banks until they reached Khimki, a northern suburb of Moscow. Bock saw in this attack a ray of hope. He recalled Hitler's latest instructions, and for a few hours he considered disengaging the remaining divisions of Fourth Army from their positions in front of the city and sending them around to the northwest in an attempt to exploit the advance. He contacted Reinhardt and Kluge to discuss the propriety of such a move. Even as Bock was in discussion with these officers, the 7th Panzer Division reported that its units were under heavy attack from Russian tanks and cavalry and considered their position across the canal to be untenable. Reluctantly, Bock granted permission for the 7th Panzer Division to withdraw, but many men and tanks of this division, including the divisional commander, failed to recross the canal and were never heard from again.

On 29 November, the vanguard of the Fourth Panzer Army and some units of the Fourth Infantry Army broke through Russian defenses and reached the western suburbs of Moscow. Some German tanks reached Tushino, which is a sector of Moscow proper. Russian soldiers and civilians, including women and children, fought the Germans from every street corner and housetop. Kluge called Bock with the information that he was fast running out of men, but proposed to launch a concerted drive on 1 December, if Bock would furnish a few additional battalions. Bock replied that he had no more battalions but urged Kluge to press the attack on 1 December, as planned, with what forces he had.

The military situation in front of Moscow was approaching its most critical phase. Bock knew that Hitler was waiting, the German nation was waiting, the whole world was waiting and watching the bitter struggle at Moscow. Again, as it had done in October, the German radio alerted the German people that a very special announcement would be made within hours. Newspapers all over the world headlined the fateful drama that was now being played at the gates of Moscow. Some predicted that Moscow was about to fall; others were more skeptical. An American weekly (*Time*) assessed the situation with considerable accuracy. "Before Moscow," it stated, "Bock is expending men and materiel whose strength Germany will never be able to call on again. . . ."[91] In the same report the periodical made a remarkable prediction: ". . . It is just possible that when the history of the Second World War is written and a list is made of the generals who have done most to whittle down Germany's chances of victory, the name of Marshal von Bock will lead all the rest. . . ."[92]

In Moscow, Josef Stalin and his Defense Committee held continuous emergency meetings. On several occasions, one or the other member suggested either a complete evacuation of the city, as Alexander I had done in 1812, or the appointment of a delegation to ask the Germans for an armistice. In each case, the suggestion was overruled by the majority. On 29 November, the Communist Party's official newspaper, *Pravda,* appeared on the bleak, cold, wind-swept streets of the city. Its headlines read: "Enemy Offensive Continues! All Citizens for the Defense of Our Capital!"[93]

An almost complete breakdown in communications now occurred between Bock's headquarters and the high German military hierarchy. It had been in the making for some weeks. The breakdown was not a practical one, for despite constant disruptions due to adverse weather, partisan activity, and the innumerable accidents that occur in modern combat, the signal troops of Army Group Center and other echelons of the German Army had worked frantically and unceasingly to maintain radio, telegraph, and telephone communications between the major commands.

Rather, the breakdown was caused by an inexplicable unwillingness on the part of Bock and the higher authorities to correctly evaluate the military situation that prevailed on the snowy fields and icy forests before the gates of Moscow. They believed that Moscow could possibly be conquered, but they refused to recognize that Moscow might *not* be conquered. They refused to permit themselves any alternatives. They refused to realize that if Moscow did not capitulate, Army Group Center would be confronted with catastrophe.

Bock was a man who was steeped in Prussian military tradition. But with regard to military operations he was also a practical man—a man rich in the experience that is derived from over forty years of active military service. He must have realized that from a military point of view the final conquest of Moscow was no longer possible. Yet Bock's vanity, ambition, and professional pride moved him to order his armies to certain disaster and his men to certain death, in futile attempts to accomplish what had now become a practical impossibility.

During late November and early December 1941, when the fate of Army Group Center and perhaps the fate of Germany teetered in the balance, Bock minced no words in his assessment of the military situation. He stated over and over again to Army High Command that the officers and men of Army Group Center had reached the end of their strength, that there were no supplies or reserve troops left to his disposal, and that it was questionable whether or not the final objective, the destruction of Russian military forces in front of Moscow and the conquest of the city, could be achieved. Nevertheless, in his most pessimistic reports, von Bock always seemed to hold out a glimmer of hope. Whether or not he did it deliberately or inadvertently and how much it influenced Hitler and the high military hierarchy remain debatable. One point, however, is irrefutable: Bock's stubborn determination, strengthened by sheer desperation, now overrode all practical military considerations.

On 30 November, the thermometer registered forty-five degrees below zero. Again Bock went to a forward command post, within sight of Moscow, where he took personal direction of his troops' painful progress, literally man by man, tank by tank, gun by gun. While there, he received a call from Army High Command. Halder's deputy, Heusinger, was on the line and informed Bock that Hitler desired to know the approximate time that the complete encirclement and destruction of enemy forces could be officially announced. Bock disdained to answer Heusinger directly, and inquired if Brauchitsch were available. Brauchitsch was still recovering from his recent heart attack but was present at his post at Army High Command. Bock demanded to talk with him.

The dialogue that ensued between Germany's highest military men manifested the low ebb of the professional leadership of the German Army in the face of impending disaster:

Bock: Will you inform the Führer that we are performing to the utmost of our ability here? The situation is indeed critical. I am using every man in the best manner I see fit. The bare truth is, I have no longer the troops at my disposal to encircle the enemy. I have committed all my reserves. Just yesterday, I brought up the 255th Security Division from Army Group Rear Area, although it is sorely needed behind the front to secure inadequate supply and communication lines.

Guderian's XLVII Corps has reached the Oka north of Ryasan, but it is doubtful if it can cross the Oka and exploit the advance in the face of strong enemy counterattacks. The 7th Panzer Division has withdrawn from its eastern bridgehead across the Moscow-Volga Canal. In the process, it lost most of its effective striking power. It is clear that the enemy is aware of our intentions, and he is concentrating fresh forces both north and south of Moscow. The presence of these fresh enemy troops, numerically superior and equipped to conduct operations in the winter weather, dangerously threatens both the southern and northern wings of my army group.

My one hope is to continue the attack frontally. In doing this, however, there exists the danger of a brutish, chest-to-chest struggle, such as occurred at Verdun twenty-five years ago. I have no desire to be a participant in that kind of struggle. I emphasize that Army Group Center is at the end of its strength.

Brauchitsch: Guderian has reached Kashira, too, has he not?

Bock: Some spearhead units have reached there. And probably Kolomna, too. But the entire attack has no depth. The men are physically exhausted. The combat strength with which to mount an offensive of the proportions that the Führer desires simply does not exist any more.

Brauchitsch: What about Kluge? Our report here states that he has broken through enemy defenses and is actually in the city.

Bock: Kluge is difficult to convince. On his own volition, he has delayed attacking several times. I have given him all available reserves. There have been some local breakthroughs, but nothing on a broad scale. And even these are being snipped off as fast as they develop. I have last night relieved a divisional commander who reported that the Russians had repulsed his men with hammers and shovels.

Brauchitsch: The Führer is convinced that the Russians are on the verge of complete collapse. He desires a definite commitment from you, Field Marshal von Bock, as to when this collapse will become a reality.

Bock: Army High Command has falsely estimated the situation here. I have reported dozens of times during the past days that the army group no longer commands the strength to force a decision. Unless we obtain ample reserve forces immediately I cannot be responsible for the outcome.

Brauchitsch: The outcome of the operation is your responsibility.

Bock: And I have discharged this responsibility by informing you of the critical situation that has developed. For many weeks now we have been begging for winter clothing and supplies. At this moment, the temperature is forty-five degrees below zero. German soldiers, dressed only in field coats, are fighting against an amply supplied enemy.

Brauchitsch: But the winter supplies have been delivered.

Bock: I wish to assure you, Field Marshal Brauchitsch, that they have not been delivered. The supply situation has been very precarious since early October. We have considered ourselves extremely fortunate if we could obtain the bare necessities for the conduct of the operation—munitions, fuel, rations. The fact that winter supplies have not arrived is to me the best indication that higher headquarters are not aware of the true situation here.

Brauchitsch: The winter supplies for Army Group Center have been underway since early October. I do not have the statistics at hand, but Wagner has taken care of that.

Bock: Statistics will show, I believe, that the necessary winter supplies for my army group are safely ensconced in storage areas and warehouses far behind the front. That is, if they exist at all. I repeat, Field Marshal Brauchitsch, a gross miscalculation has been made. Army High Command, and the Führer as well, have unfortunately overestimated the situation. . . . Brauchitsch, are you still there? Hello! Has the connection been cut? Brauchitsch, are you listening?

Brauchitsch: What were you saying, Bock?

Bock: I said that higher headquarters has miscalculated. Please inform the Führer that Army Group Center is no longer in the position to achieve its objective. We do not have the strength any more. Are you listening, Brauchitsch?

Brauchitsch: Yes, I am listening. The Führer wishes to know when Moscow will fall.

Bock: Are you aware of what is happening here? Are you aware of the fact that future events will have to take their own course? That they have surpassed the realm of military decision and are now of a political nature? Army Group Center is no longer able to force the issue.

Brauchitsch: You have ordered a new attack, have you not? When will it take place?[94]

Bock recorded later that he had not trusted his own hearing, and for some hours he found it difficult to believe that the man to whom he had been talking was his colleague of many years. For some time afterward, Bock was visibly affected by his conversation with Brauchitsch.

Later during the afternoon, word reached Army Group Center that Field Marshal Kesselring and two air corps of his Air Fleet 2 were being transferred to North Africa, where German and Italian forces had suffered a severe setback at the hands of the English in Libya. The one air corps left to Army Group Center was to be commanded by Lieutenant General von Richthofen.[95] Bock was reluctant to lose the services of his trusted friend, Kesselring. But he did not protest the transfer. His reasoning was that, in any case, the severely cold weather on his front had rendered aircraft practically inoperable in the battle for Moscow.

The next day found Bock still deliberating over his traumatic conversation with Brauchitsch. He concluded that in spite of all that had been said, Army High Command still had no clear picture of the military situation. He decided to send another telegram to Army High Command:

In the face of all dangers and with totally exhausted troops I am attempting to continue the attack. From a tactical point of view, however, only frontal assaults are possible. The combat strength of the Army Group permits no classical movements of encirclement. The attack now in progress will gain some ground but at bloody costs. It will destroy some of the enemy, but it will not force a decision. . . . Any concept at higher headquarters that the enemy is collapsing is, as the events of the last days will show, only a wild dream. The enemy now has numerical superiority before the gates of Moscow.... Even if the improbable takes place, and my troops enter the city, it is doubtful if they can hold it. The attack therefore appears to be without purpose, the troops have lost confidence, and the time is nearing when they will be able to do no more. What happens after that remains to be decided. My army group at this time is spread over a front almost 700 miles wide. It has no more reserve divisions. ...

I am unaware of the views of higher headquarters. If, however, it is decided to revert to a war of defense during this winter, I request that sufficient reserve forces be obtained to permit time for the exhausted troops on the front to recuperate. A minimum of twenty divisions would be needed for this purpose. I do not know if they are available, and if available, I doubt if they can be brought to the front in time to execute such a plan. ...

Above all, the supply situation must be brought to a condition of order and reliability. If this is not possible, then we must not lose time in establishing a shortened line of defense, so that Army Group Center may be ready to fight another day.

Bock

Field Marshal[96]

There was no direct reply to Bock's communication. On the next day, 3 December, Halder called and stated that any overestimation or miscalculation of the situation on Army Group Center's front existed not at Army High Command but at Hitler's headquarters. Determined now to leave nothing to chance with regard to his position, Bock thereupon attempted to contact Hitler directly. Hitler was not available, so Bock talked to Colonel General Alfred Jodl, Chief of Operations, Armed Forces High Command. He repeated in essence what he had often told Brauchitsch, orally and in writing, during the past days. But in conclusion Bock added: "Despite the adverse circumstances I have not given up hope. There remains the remote possibility of conquering the city of Moscow. *The last battalion will decide the issue!*"[97] With this last remark, Bock again falsely estimated the military situation. Whether or not he did this deliberately or inadvertently is unknown.

On 4 December, units of the Second Army forced their way into Kuntsevo, a southeastern suburb of Moscow. Although there was no organized defense of the area in the military sense, the city's inhabitants—men, women, and often children—fought a guerrilla-type, street-by-street, house-by-house engagement against the exhausted German veterans, as they had done at Tushino. For awhile, it appeared that the Germans would break through the numerous barricades that the Russian defenders had thrown up and would gain entry into the city itself. A few German squads of tanks and infantry did reach the frozen Moscow River, which runs through southeastern Moscow. From there they could see the Kremlin. But their ammunition gave out, and the Germans withdrew, leaving behind their dead and wounded, the latter to be slaughtered by the infuriated Russians.

On the same day Guderian's forces reached the suburbs of Tula. Other units of Guderian's army bypassed Kolomna and battled their way to the Moscow River. In the north, the Third Panzer Army's tanks again fought into Khimki, a Moscow suburb. They, too, turned back after exhausting their ammunition and fuel supplies.

These were the last advances that the forces of Army Group Center made under Bock's command. There were not many survivors of the last German attempts to seize the Communist capital. Of those who were still alive after the Second World War, some have said that final victory may have hung on a single artillery shell, a frozen tank engine that refused to run, a broken tank track, a malfunctioning machine gun, or perhaps a slain, brave officer or noncommissioned officer, whose death at a critical moment demoralized further the living.[98]

On 6 December, the temperature stood at an incredible fifty degrees below zero. On this day, Russian reserve forces, commanded by the capable Zhukov, launched a tremendous, well-timed counterattack against Bock's exhausted forces all along the Moscow front. Guderian called Bock and stated that he had cancelled all attacks and had instructed his divisions—or what remained of them—to destroy whatever equipment they could not carry with them and to withdraw to the Don River. Kluge called, too, to report that Russian pressure was intolerable and that Fourth Army had reverted to defense in the entire sector. Weichs reported himself ill and said that Russian troops had broken through in several critical places and that both he and Second Army·were on the verge of collapse.

Bock assigned command of the Second Army to Lieutenant General Rudolf Schmidt. Reinhardt reported that his tank units were withdrawing from the Moscow-Volga Canal under pressure of heavy enemy attacks. Hoepner could not be reached, but reports indicated that the Fourth Panzer Army was also in retreat from its overextended positions. In all cases, German troops were abandoning their tanks whose motors refused to run and their light and heavy guns whose frozen recoil mechanisms refused to function, and were making their way in the best manner they could through the bitter cold and high snowdrifts back to defense positions. They did not run, for that was impossible in the frozen Russian terrain. They did not rout or panic, for there was no more energy left even for that. They simply plodded and trudged along until they were out of the range of the counterattacking Russians' artillery and rocket fire. Some found cover in Russian village dwellings and farmhouses, where they managed to survive the bitter cold.

Others floundered in the deep snow, either sobbing bitterly or cursing their fate, until they fell and quickly froze to death. Even the slightest incapacitating wound from enemy fire meant death from freezing, for no aid was forthcoming.

In the evening reports that reached Bock's headquarters, he noted that some of his units had intercepted enemy radio conversations and instructions in the English language. This development was as disconcerting to Bock as all the other bad news. "Are the English or Americans helping the Russians, too?" he pondered. He directed that any reports of captured English-speaking soldiers and the results of their interrogation be sent immediately to his headquarters.[99]

Other reports from reconnaissance planes that somehow had managed to survive flights over the areas east and south of Moscow indicated that the Russians were concentrating large forces around Alexandrov, Orechevo, and Ryasan. Meanwhile, the Russian counterattack mounted in intensity. Later in the evening Bock again telephoned Halder and informed him of the latest developments. He stated that he had given freedom of decision to his commanders to conduct operations according to their best judgment. The troops could attack no more. Field Marshal von Bock's mighty, ill-fated attempt to conquer Moscow in 1941, upon which the Nazi German nation had staked so much, had come to an end.

By evening of 7 December, it was apparent that Marshal Zhukov's counterattack had made serious ruptures all along the front and that the Russians were advancing at will. The Russians had waited until the exact moment when Bock's men had expended their last ounce of energy and had fired practically their last round of ammunition. Now they poured through great gaps in the German positions, fighting their own blitzkrieg operation of encirclement and destruction and threatening to cut off the overextended Germans. In the north, they recaptured Kalinin and, using skis and sleighs to move their equipment, struck at Rshev. Several divisions of the Third Panzer Army were overrun. In the central sector, the Russians crossed the frozen Moscow, Rusa, and Lama rivers; drove the Germans out of Volokolamsk, Staritsa, and Lotochino; and forced a wide breakthrough in the area controlled by Ninth Army. In the south, they struck westward on either side of Kaluga with great force and hemmed in large numbers of Guderian's army east of Tula.

On 8 December, the German Armed Forces High Command announced tersely: "Due to the onset of Russian winter the operations in the East are being curtailed. On most parts of the East Front only local engagements are taking place."[100]

Helplessly, Bock followed the developments. Desperately, he sent urgent telegrams to Army High Command. Sadly, he rejected the plaintive calls for help from his senior commanders, from Reinhardt and Hoepner, from Kluge and Schmidt, from Guderian and Strauss. There were no more troops left to fill the gaps in their lines. While earlier, regiments and divisions had disintegrated before the Russian onslaughts and the terrible weather, now armies were disintegrating. Army Group Center was disintegrating. Dejectedly, Bock sat at his lonely desk and penned a long summarization of what had happened and what was happening:

It seems to me that three factors have led to the present difficult crisis. The first was the muddy autumn season. We could not exploit the great victories at Vyasma and Bryansk because the movement of troops and supplies was seriously hindered by the mud.

The second factor was the breakdown of the entire supply system. The primitive highway and railway system in Russia prevented the proper utilization of our mechanized and motorized forces. This resulted in a shortage of fuel, a shortage of railway cars and locomotives, the inability to change quickly enough to the Russian railroad gauge, the mechanical failure of thousands of vehicles, which were built to operate on good roads. Added to this was the perennial shortage of qualified personnel to operate the supply system. Also, there must be considered the fact that our equipment, mechanized and railway, was not constructed to withstand the hardships of the severe Russian weather. . . .

Finally, we underestimated the strength of the enemy, his ability to recuperate after suffering losses that would have toppled almost any other nation, and his great reserves in manpower and materiel. . . .

The Russians understood all along what difficulties we were having with transportation and supply. They placed much emphasis on disruption and destruction of our supply lines. They were successful, for the dire necessities with which to conduct military operations never reached the front. . . .

Despite the great handicaps under which my soldiers have fought, they have accomplished much. Despite an absence of a properly functioning supply and communications system, they have advanced eastward a distance of over 800 miles, traversing some of the most difficult terrain on this earth. There are no words to describe their bravery, their superhuman efforts, their devotion, their willingness to give their lives in the cause of the Fatherland. . . .

And here we are today, faced with a situation from which we cannot extract ourselves, cannot maneuver, and cannot repel an enemy who throws masses of men at us without regard to losses. It is no wonder that my soldiers ask themselves: "What have we done to deserve this?"

In a surprisingly short time, the Russians have regrouped their defeated divisions, have brought new, fresh ones from Siberia, from the Iranian border, from the Caucasus. They have substituted the very effective rocket launcher for their lost artillery. . . .

Today there are twenty-four more Russian divisions in front of my army group than there were on 15 November. These new divisions confront German troops who have fought for months and months without cessation, who have endured indescribable hardships in the cause of the Fatherland. My troops have given all they have; they can do no more. Their supreme efforts are reflected in the shockingly high losses among both commanders and men. . . .

All along, I demanded of Army High Command the authority to strike down the enemy when he was wobbling. We could have finished the enemy last summer. We could have destroyed him completely. Last August, the road to Moscow was open; we could have entered the Bolshevik capital in triumph and in summery weather. The high military leadership of the Fatherland made a terrible mistake when it forced my army group to adopt a position of defense last August. Now all of us are paying for that mistake. . . .[101]

Later on that momentous day, 8 December, Bock noted that the Japanese had attacked the American naval base at Pearl Harbor and destroyed a large part of the U.S. Navy. "This will certainly widen the war. The Americans now have a legal basis for assisting the English and Russians, which they have been doing all along. How different would things be if the Japanese had attacked the Russians."[102]

During the next days the military situation rapidly worsened. Bock spent much time in further desperate communication with Halder, with Brauchitsch, and with representatives at Hitler's headquarters advising them of the perilous situation and that Army Group Center was about to collapse. He begged for reinforcements and was told that four divisions were being flown from France to help. "Too little and too late!" lamented Bock.[103]

Nonetheless, Bock made determined efforts to save what remained of his army group. He exhorted commanders to put forth every effort to block the enemy's attacks, to close the most obvious gaps, to rescue trapped German units, and to bolster the most apparent points of weakness. In some instances, desperately fighting German soldiers succeeded in halting the Russian attacks and stabilizing their lines. It was ironical that the severe weather that had played a large part in preventing the Germans from achieving their objective now helped to save them from complete disaster. On 10 December, still another fierce blizzard struck the area. This slowed the Russian attacks. If it was difficult for the Germans to move over the impassable terrain, it was equally difficult for the Russians, despite the fact that they were better equipped for the winter.

By 13 December, however, six days after the Russian counterattack began, the German forces had retreated more than fifty miles. Moscow was no longer within their grasp. On the same day, after repeated delays due to the bad weather and a very rapid increase in partisan activity behind the German lines, Field Marshal von Brauchitsch finally arrived by special airplane at Bock's headquarters. This was the first meeting between the two officers in over two months, and it was an unpleasant affair. Bock summarized in detail the situation, outlining the locations of the Russian breakthroughs, and emphasizing that Army Group Center could no longer resist the Russian attacks. He suggested that Army Group Center withdraw to a defense line running through Gomel-Mogilev-Vitebsk, to recuperate, obtain reinforcements, and prepare to resume the campaign in the following spring. Bock concluded his summary with these words: "Other than those I have already made, I have no more proposals to make. The decisions now to be made transcend the military."[104]

Brauchitsch was gaunt and wan from his recent serious illness. He listened carefully and agreed in substance with Bock but reminded him that since the situation transcended the military he was not in a position to authorize a withdrawal to the defense line that Bock had suggested. More-over, Brauchitsch stated, he was quite certain that Hitler would not agree to such a withdrawal, which would mean yielding a large part of Russian territory that had been con-quered. For the next hours, two of Germany's highest and most skilled professional soldiers argued and debated the fate of Army Group Center. Finally, Brauchitsch decided that he would travel on the next morning to other com-manders in the army group to obtain their views. After some discussion of this point, he decided to visit von Kluge and Guderian. Both officers were contacted by radio and were requested to meet Brauchitsch at Roslavl.

Later, after Brauchitsch had retired for the evening, Bock thought about how physically ill and spiritually broken Brauchitsch appeared to be. Bock wondered how long he himself would be able to withstand the physical and mental strain of the past weeks. He had been seriously ill a year ago; he feared that in the circumstances the illness might recur. Field Marshal von Bock decided that on the next morning he would request to be relieved from command of Army Group Center.[105]

But on the next morning Bock reconsidered. He decided to await the results of Brauchitsch's visit to Kluge and Guderian. He did not accompany Brauchitsch, preferring to remain in general contact with as many of his units as was possible from his own headquarters. Besides, Schmundt, Hitler's adjutant, had sent word that he was trying to reach Bock's headquarters, and he hoped to arrive that day.

At about noon, Schmundt arrived by train, after ex-periencing several delays. Again Bock repeated his estimates to Schmundt, who also agreed that the military situation was extremely critical and perhaps not fully understood at Hit-ler's headquarters. The two men decided to await Brau-chitsch's return before contacting Hitler.

Long after darkness Brauchitsch returned to Bock's headquarters, and the three officers sat down to a conference. Brauchitsch stated that both Kluge and Guderian were in accord with Bock's views. At Bock's insistence, Schmundt called Hitler's headquarters in East Prussia and informed Jodl of the situation. Jodl promised to inform Hitler and obtain a decision. Within an hour, the long distance telephone jingled in Bock's headquarters. Hitler was calling. He talked only to Schmundt, and stated that only limited withdrawals were authorized; that is, only those that were necessary to "shorten the lines."[106]

On the next day, Brauchitsch departed for the long, treacherous journey back to Germany. Schmundt remained for a day longer and spent his time at Bock's headquarters, closely following the efforts of Bock and his senior staff officers to contrive ways and means to save Army Group Center by "limited withdrawals." The Russians, however, were not cooperative. The blizzard of the past days had ceased, and the Russians renewed their attacks, making several more breakthroughs in Second Panzer Army's and Fourth Army's areas. Again Schmundt called Hitler, who, when advised that Bock was issuing orders to evacuate installations along the front, stated: "I require Field Marshal von Bock to issue the following instructions to the organizations in his command: Stand and fight! Not another yard backward!"[107]

Early on the next morning, Schmundt left Bock's headquarters, the weather having cleared sufficiently to permit travel by airplane. On the evening of the same day, Schmundt called from Hitler's headquarters. He talked to Bock's chief of staff, Greiffenberg, and informed him that Hitler had relieved Brauchitsch of command of the German Army and had himself assumed command. Bock was to deal henceforth directly with Hitler.

The situation had now reached an impasse. Army Group Center continued to disintegrate as a military organization, and Bock decided to appeal to Schmundt again. They conducted a long discussion of the same nature as when Schmundt was at Bock's headquarters. Finally, Bock wanted to know if Hitler had been appraised of the situation as Schmundt himself had seen it during his recent visit. Schmundt's answer was that Hitler had many things on his mind, and he was not sure if he was aware of every aspect of Army Group Center's position, because he had not been consistently and correctly informed. Schmundt added that this was probably unfortunate, because now that Hitler had assumed command of the German Army, it was necessary for him to be well informed of operational details.

To this Bock replied: "As you know, Schmundt, my health hangs on a silken thread. If Hitler believes that a new commander is needed here, I am in accord with his belief. But I would wish that my personal position not enter into this decision. Here in the vast Russian space individuals and their personal considerations should not matter. The situation is such that no single man can save it, anyway. Please inform Hitler of what I have said."[108]

At 12:30 A. M., 17 December, Bock was aroused by an aide. Hitler was calling:

Schmundt has informed me of the conversation between you and him. As I have stated before, my concept for the winter campaign is that to withdraw to unprepared defense positions, leaving behind artillery and heavy equipment, is inappropriate and invites disaster. Since this is true, the only alternative is not to retreat at all. As you also know, I have personally assumed command of the army, and I intend to assist Army Group Center in holding its lines. I have ordered the air force to bring reinforcements to Army Group Center with the utmost speed.

Bock replied to Hitler: "All of my instructions have been issued in the sense which you mention. But it is my duty to inform you that, because of the dangerous situation in which Army Group Center finds itself, the possibility exists that the front will be crushed."

Hitler was not to be dissuaded. "That is a risk we must take," he told Bock.[109]

On 18 December, Keitel placed a long distance telephone call to von Bock. Keitel stated that since Bock had mentioned his failing health several times in the recent past, perhaps it would be better if he took an extended leave.

Bock replied that he had no objection to taking leave for health reasons, but demanded to know if there were other motives behind this development, such as an allegation of dereliction of duty or incompetence. Keitel replied that the decision had been made by Hitler, and there were no ulterior motives involved in it. "If it will clarify matters," stated Keitel, "I will repeat the Führer's exact words: 'After Bock's severe illness of last year, and the strain that this campaign has demanded of him, I can understand why he is ill again. I would like Bock to be assured that he will be given a chance to recover.' "[110]

Late in the evening of 18 December, von Kluge arrived at Headquarters, Army Group Center. He greeted Bock with the information that he had come to "represent" him at the army group. Bock prepared to take his departure. On 19 December, at 11:30 A. M. there was a short ceremony at the headquarters, in which about twenty-five staff officers of Army Group Center participated. After the ceremony, Bock expressed farewell to each individual officer, wished him a happy holiday season in the circumstances, and enjoined him to remain steadfast and loyal to his duties. "Better times will come, my trusted colleagues!" Bock concluded.[111]

Bock then departed Army Group Center for the last time. He traveled by automobile over the difficult and treacherous route back to Germany, accompanied by his personal aides-de-camp, Hardenberg and Lehndorff. He spent the night of 19 December in Minsk and the night of 20 December in Vilna. Late on the evening of 21 December, Bock walked into Hitler's offices. "The Führer greeted me, as usual, in a friendly manner," Bock noted. "He spoke knowledgeably of the situation and expressed regret that he had not always received Army Group Center's reports in the form in which I had transmitted them. . . . I used the opportunity to urge upon the Führer the necessity for revamping the entire supply system in the German Army and assured him that when this is done the German Army can successfully complete the Russian campaign in the coming year. Upon departure, I asked the Führer if I could inform him when I have recovered from the strain of the past weeks. He answered: 'Yes, by all means.' "[112]

Bock then resumed his journey to Berlin. Arriving in the German capital, he noted that the people of Berlin seemed in general far more subdued and resigned than they had been when he was there in the previous spring. On Christmas Day 1941, Bock placed a call from Berlin to Greiffenberg at headquarters, Army Group Center. The two officers exchanged holiday greetings, after which Greiffenberg informed Bock that the situation was still almost unbearable, and, moreover, Kluge was advising the staff that he was commanding Army Group Center, rather than "representing" Bock. Greiffenberg asked Bock to obtain clarification as to who was in fact commanding the army group.

This was disconcerting news for Bock. For the moment, it did not matter that the military conquest of Moscow, in which he had played perhaps the most prominent role, had failed, and a turning point in the war had been reached. It did not particularly matter that over a quarter of a million German soldiers lay dead on the battlefields between Brest-Litovsk and Moscow. It did not matter that Army Group Center was still fighting for its life on the vast, frozen ex-

panses in front of Moscow. What mattered to Bock was
Bock.

He called Halder and demanded to know who was in fact
commanding Army Group Center—Bock or Kluge? Halder
promised to investigate and return the call.

But Halder did not call. During the next days Bock had
no official contact with anyone in the German Army High
Command. He learned through his aides-de-camp that
twenty-one generals in his former command had been sent
home, including Guderian and Hoepner.

On New Year's Day 1942, Lieutenant General Bodewin
Keitel, Chief of the Personnel Office, Armed Forces High
Command, and brother of Field Marshal Wilhelm Keitel,
came to see Bock. Bodewin Keitel was obviously calling at
the behest of Hitler. He informed Bock that Hitler had decided, in view of the difficult circumstances, to leave Kluge
in command of Army Group Center. However, Hitler
wished Bock to know that his official position was a "member of the Führer's reserve."

Bock asked if this meant retirement, and Keitel answered:
"Absolutely not. You are at the Führer's disposal, and you
will probably be asked to accept a high active post in the
very near future."[113]

Somewhat assured, Field Marshal von Bock spent the
next days in his Berlin apartment, pondering his and Germany's future in the difficult months to come.

1. A. M. Samsonov, *Velikaya Bitva pod Moskvoi* (Moscow, 1958), pp. 51–56. 2. *Ibid.*

3. German military slang meaning Stalin's organ, because of the fearful screeching and moaning made by the incoming rockets. This very effective weapon is mentioned in almost every account of the German-Russian war. There seems to be no evidence that the Germans knew of the rocket launcher's existence, however, until the Russians used it in large quantities against Bock's forces in October 1941. See H. Gp. Mitte KTB, microfilm no. 226/65002/75/438 (Washington, D.C.: U.S. National Archives, n.d.).

4. Von Bock KTB, 21–26 September 1941. 5. *Ibid.*, 28 September 1941.

6. Guderian, pp. 208–10.

7. Tippelskirch, pp. 238–40. 8. *Ibid.*

9. Germany, 1950. Personal interview with a former soldier of the Wehrmacht.

10. There are many accounts of Hitler's order of the day on 2 October 1941. See Tippelskirch, p. 234; H. G. Greiner, *Die Oberste Wehrmachtsführung: 1939-1943* (Wiesbaden, 1953), p. 141; *New York Times,* 3 October 1941, p. 8; and others.

11. Von Bock KTB, 2 October 1941.

12. Halder KTB, III, 2 October 1941, p. 263.

13. Von Bock KTB, 2 October 1941.

14. This account, one of many relating to Hitler's dramatic address, is taken from *Deutscher Beamten-Kalender: 1941* (Berlin, 1942), p. 93.

15. Guderian, p. 209.

16. Von Bock KTB, 3 October 1941. 17. *Ibid.* 18. 4 October 1941.

19. Samsonov, p. 89; Shilin, pp. 134–36; and S. P. Platanov, N. G. Pavlenko, and I. V. Parotkin (eds.), *Vtoraya Miravaya Voina,* vol. I (Moscow, 1958), p. 196.

20. Tippelskirch, p. 233.

21. Germany, 1949. Interviews with Johann Ertelt, a former soldier of the German Wehrmacht.

22. Von Bock KTB, 5 October 1941. 23. *Ibid.*

24. Halder KTB, III, 5 October 1941, pp. 267–79.

25. Von Bock KTB, 6 October 1941. 26. *Ibid.* 27. *Ibid.* 28. *Ibid.*

29. *Ibid.*, 7 October 1941. The italics are Bock's.   30. *Ibid.*

31. Germany, 1951. Personal interview with Guderian.

32. H. Gp. Mitte KTB, microfilm no. 289/26974/17–19/63 (Washington, D.C.: U.S. National Archives, n.d.).

33. Von Bock KTB, 8 October 1941. Bock devotes considerable space in his diary to an analysis of Hitler's direct instructions.   34. *Ibid.*

35. *Ibid.* Halder mentions Bock's telegram in his war diary but makes no reference to Bock's exact words. Bock states, however, that he received assurances from Halder that his headquarters would not interfere again with Bock's conduct of the war, although he could not predict Hitler's actions. See Halder KTB, III, 9 October 1941, p. 181.

36. Germany, 1950. Personal interview with Josef Gessner, a former soldier in the Wehrmacht.

37. Von Bock KTB, 9 October 1941.

38. *Ibid.*, 11 October 1941. Halder, who was soon to become ill and go on sick leave for several weeks, is noncommittal about this episode and devotes three words to it in his diary: *Weiterführung der Operation* (continuation of the operation). See Halder KTB, 11 October 1941.

39. H. Gp. Mitte KTB, microfilm no. 289/26974/17–19/88–91 (Washington, D.C.: U.S. National Archives, n.d.).

40. Von Bock KTB, 11 October 1941.

41. Quoted from Samsonov, pp. 107–08.

42. Germany, 1950. Personal interviews with Frau Katherine von Hahn, a former resident of Berlin.

43. *Der Völkische Beobachter,* 12 October 1941.

44. Germany, 1952. Personal interview. See n. 42.   45. *Ibid.*

46. Samsonov, p. 94.   47. *Ibid.*, p. 96.

48. Kurt Zentner, *Lehren und Bilder aus dem Russlandfeldzug: 1941–1945* (Hamburg, 1952), p. 45.

49. Samsonov, pp. 103–04.

50. Von Bock KTB, 13 October 1941.

51. H. Gp. Mitte KTB, microfilm no. 288/75854/643 (Washington, D.C.: U.S. National Archives, n.d.).

52. Guderian, pp. 215–16.

53. Von Bock KTB, 19 October 1941.

54. *Der Völkische Beobachter,* 16 October 1941.

55. Von Bock KTB, 19 October 1941. 56. *Ibid.*, 20 October 1941.

57. Josef Saal, as quoted in the *Frankfurter Zeitung*, 21 October 1941.

58. *Der Völkische Beobachter*, 21 October 1941.

59. H. Gp. Mitte KTB, microfilm no. 288/75854/667 (Washington, D.C.: U.S. National Archives, n.d.).

60. Von Bock KTB, 22 October 1941. 61. *Ibid.*

62. Von Bock KTB, 23, 24, and 25 October 1941. There seems to be no record of what was discussed during these visits. It is probable that in Himmler's case, however, the discussion centered on the conduct and performance of Waffen-SS units under Bock's command.

63. *Ibid.* 64. 26 October 1941.

65. H. Gp. Mitte KTB, microfilm no. 215/26974/33/908 (Washington, D.C.: U.S. National Archives, n.d.). Total German casualties, excluding sick, in the Russian campaign from its beginning to 10 November 1941 were about 700,000. Bock's losses were always heavier than those of Army Groups North and South. See Halder KTB, III, 11 November 1941, p. 287.

66. Von Bock KTB, 26 October 1941. 67. *Ibid.*, 27 October 1941.

68. Halder was hospitalized or convalescing during the period, and there are no entries in his war diary from 10 October to 3 November 1941. See Halder KTB, III, pp. 266–67.

69. Von Bock KTB, 29 October 1941. See also Guderian, p. 222.

70. Von Bock KTB, 29 October 1941.

71. *Ibid.*, 30 October 1941. 72. *Ibid.* 73. *Ibid.* 74. *Ibid.* 75. *Ibid.*

76. *Ibid.*, 2 November 1941. In late November, however, the Chief of Military Administration, Army Group Center, presented a plaque to von Bock on behalf of the city of Smolensk and its "liberation from Bolshevism." See H. Gp. Mitte KTB, microfilm no. 233/75858/581 (Washington, D.C.: U.S. National Archives, n.d.).

77. Von Bock KTB, 5 November 1941.

78. Guderian, p. 223.

79. Von Bock KTB, 10 November 1941.

80. H. Gp. Mitte KTB, microfilm no. 233/75860/742 (Washington, D.C.: U.S. National Archives, n.d.).

81. Von Bock KTB, 10 November 1941. 82. *Ibid.* 83. 11 November 1941.

84. Carell, pp. 163–64.

85. Von Bock KTB, 14 November 1941. Bock also recorded on that

day that casualties due to freezing were averaging about 400 a day.

86. Guderian, p. 228, and Von Bock KTB, 15 November 1941.

87. Von Bock KTB, 18 November 1941.

88. *Ibid.* 89. 20 November 1941. 90. *Ibid.*

91. *Time,* 1 December 1941. 92. *Ibid.*

93. *Pravda,* 29 November 1941.

94. Von Bock KTB, 30 November 1941.

95. This was the VIII Air Corps. See von Bock KTB, 30 November 1941, and Albert Kesselring, *Erinnerungen* (Heidelberg, 1952), p. 184.

96. Von Bock KTB, 1 December 1941.

97. *Ibid.,* 3 December 1941. Italics supplied.

98. Germany, 1950. Personal interview with Major General Helmuth von Sanne, a former staff officer in Army Group Center.

99. Von Bock KTB, 8 December 1941.

100. *Kriegstagebuch des Oberkommandos der Wehrmacht,* vol. I (Frankfurt, 1965), p. 1210.

101. Von Bock KTB, 8 December 1941. 102. *Ibid.*

103. *Ibid.,* 10 December 1941. 104. 13 December 1941.

105. *Ibid.* 106. 14 December 1941.

107. *Ibid.,* 15 December 1941. 108. 16 December 1941. 109. 17 December 1941. 110. 18 December 1941. 111. 19 December 1941.

112. *Ibid.,* 22 December 1941. 113. 1 January 1942.

V. THE FALL OF VON BOCK

IN EARLY JANU-

ary 1942 Bock wrote a letter to Schmundt, Hitler's personal adjutant, with whom he had spent considerable time during the hectic, despairing days of December 1941, when Army Group Center floundered before the gates of Moscow. Bock took pains to be cordial in his letter, but he admitted frankly that he was still puzzled about his current status in the German Army and wished to know, in view of the "curtailment of operations because of the onset of winter on the Eastern Front,"[1] if the Führer considered Bock to have been negligent or incompetent in the execution of his duties. On 6 January, Bock received an equally cordial but somewhat vague reply. Schmundt reiterated that to the best of his knowledge Hitler had no intention of bringing any formal allegation against Bock. He added that since Hitler had now assumed command of the German Army he was very much engaged in acquainting himself with the tactical aspects of the German Army's commitments not only in Russia, but in North Africa, the Balkans, Western Europe, and the Scandinavian countries. Schmundt concluded with a statement that had become familiar to Bock during past days: "You remain at the Führer's disposal."[2]

How long Bock would have remained "at the Führer's disposal" is unknown, had not an event occurred on 15 January that directly affected him. On that date Field Marshal Walther Freiherr von Reichenau, who had assumed command of Army Group South when von Rundstedt was relieved in November 1941, suffered a severe heart attack. Reichenau died two days later. On 16 January, Bock received a call from Brigadier General Gerhard von Drabich of the Personnel Office, Armed Forces High Command. Drabich stated that his instructions were to determine if Field Marshal von Bock could immediately assume command of Army Group South. Bock replied that he would like to have fifteen minutes to consider the matter. In fifteen minutes, he telephoned Drabich and stated that he stood ready, as always, to render service to Germany and especially now in Germany's critical hour. He had therefore decided to take command of Army Group South and was available at once. He was then asked to report to Hitler at his headquarters, the Wolf's Lair, near Rastenburg, East Prussia, on the next day.

Bock's concern at that time for Germany and her deteriorating condition can perhaps best be summarized by his description of the journey by train from Berlin to East Prussia. "The sleeping car was dirty and unheated. A large number of Spanish Army officers rode in the train; they were apparently traveling to their military assignments in Russia. How embarrassing it was that they must see that we can no longer keep our trains clean! Besides, the thing was far off schedule—a hitherto unheard of event in Germany!"[3]

Hitler received Bock in the usual friendly, solicitous manner that had characterized relationships between the two men in the past. He inquired of Bock's health, to which Bock replied that he was feeling very well. He then summarized the general situation for Bock, emphasizing that by his iron-willed "Stand and Fight! No Retreat!" order he, and he alone, had saved the German forces in Russia. Hitler conceded that although the situation in the northern and central sectors of the Eastern Front was still vacillatory, the situation in Army Group South's area was, by contrast, quite stable. Army Group South held a front from Taganrog on the Azov Sea to Kursk and had given up little or no ground since the Russians had launched their "winter campaign." Bock replied that the situation in Army Group South was indeed laudatory, especially in view of the deplorable transportation system in Russia.

"The transportation system will receive due attention," was Hitler's statement. He turned to his great war map and traced with his finger a huge circle that took in all of the Russian Ukraine, the Caucasus, and the Russian territory east and north of the Caspian Sea. Hitler then gave von Bock a penetrating stare:

The war against the Bolsheviks must be brought to a successful conclusion this year. I have never been for one moment convinced that the conquest of the central and northern areas of Bolshevik Russia was the key to victory, though I condescended to my generals when they proposed to conquer Leningrad and Moscow. Since the planned conquest of Leningrad and Moscow has not yet materialized, it is obvious that a change of strategy is required.

I have come, therefore, to the difficult decision that the Bolshevik military forces must be destroyed in the Ukraine and the Caucasus. In the process, we will seize the oil-producing areas of the Caucasus, and the granaries of the Ukraine, and we will thereby cripple the Bolshevik's economy to the extent that they will have to give up the fight.... Moreover, by seizing these vital areas we will foil the attempts of the English and Americans to aid the Bolsheviks.... I am charging you, Field Marshal von Bock, with the responsibility for executing this great task....[4]

Bock was, as usual, aloof and unbending, even in Hitler's presence. But he saw in Hitler's plans a chance to redeem himself, and he readily accepted the "great task." Later, as if to belie rumors and reports that were afloat throughout Germany that Hitler had dismissed all of his experienced generals and a serious crisis in military leadership had developed, Hitler posed with Bock for press photographers and directed his press officers to display the photographs across the land. The photographs showed Bock, resplendent in his marshal's uniform, towering over Hitler and his entourage. But all were smiling warmly.[5]

Bock spent the night at Hitler's headquarters. Later he confided to his diary: "This sounds all very well, and I hope it goes well. But I think the Führer is too optimistic."[6]

On 19 January, Bock flew from Rastenburg to the headquarters of Army Group South at Poltava, 800 miles distant. At the Poltava airfield he was met by one of his former senior commanders in Army Group Center, Colonel General Hoth, who was acting commander of Army Group South, pending Bock's arrival. Hoth was worried and wasted no time in telling Bock that the situation was serious, that the Russians had broken through German lines at several places on the Donets River, mainly at Isyum, Voltshansk, and Byelgorod. Bock and Hoth reviewed the entire military situation in Army Group South, and Bock discovered —not surprisingly—that it was considerably less favorable than Hitler had pictured it at his headquarters. It was, in fact, grave.

On 20 January, Bock officially assumed command of Army Group South in a short ceremony. The army commanders and senior staff officers were present. Immediately, he busied himself with organizing his vast command according to his own concepts. Under the pressure of the Russian attacks, this was at best a difficult process. Army Group South consisted of three infantry armies—the Sixth, Eleventh, and Seventeenth—and one tank army—the First. Its air power was furnished by Air Fleet 4. Under the command of Field Marshal von Rundstedt, Army Group South had begun the Russian campaign in June 1941 with forty divisions, or about 600,000 men. These were supported by Italian, Rumanian, Hungarian, Bulgarian, and Croatian troops, although during the first six months of the Russian campaign only the Rumanians and Italians had furnished any significant combat strength. The troops of the other nations that were allied to Nazi Germany in the Russian campaign—the Hungarians, Bulgarians, and Croats—were used mainly in the rear areas to secure and maintain supply lines and to perform similar functions.[7]

Army Group South had suffered heavy casualties, though they were not as heavy as those of Army Group Center. But neither had Army Group South made as much progress. Bock resolved to resume the offensive as soon as conditions permitted, remembering that Hitler had given him the responsibility of destroying the Russian military forces in the southern areas. So, he rejected all suggestions and overtures of his subordinate commanders to withdraw to new lines under pressure of the Russian counterattacks. Having learned lessons from his experience with the Russians farther to the north, Bock exhorted his armies, corps, and divisions to concentrate all available artillery fire and air bombardment on the attacking Russians, assuring all doubters that the Russians were particularly vulnerable to heavy firepower, because of their tendency to attack with great masses of infantry.

The Russian winter had by now struck with full fury in the Ukraine and Donets-Don basins, as it had done weeks earlier around Moscow. On the day that Bock arrived in Poltava it was thirty degrees below zero at the airfield. To Bock, it was a familiar scene: the icy winds, the bleak fields, and snow-bound roads, which hampered movement of any kind. But Field Marshal von Bock noted with some satisfaction that large amounts of winter clothing had arrived, and were still arriving, for his soldiers. The German Army had been totally unprepared for the Russian winter, and the arrival of winter clothing had been the result of a frantically organized, but effective campaign in Germany to collect clothing items from every civilian source for the freezing soldiers on the East Front.[8] And although the soldierly von Bock flinched at the sight of German soldiers arrayed in Persian lamb coats, multi-colored sweaters and red ear muffs, he found consolation, at least, in the knowledge that they were as warmly clad as possible.[9]

There was yet another notable difference between Bock's conduct of the campaign in Southern Russia and the previous campaign in 1941. Bock now reported directly to Hitler. He telephoned Hitler at least once every two or three days to summarize the tactical situation or to inform Hitler of what actions he had taken or planned to take. As was his wont, Bock was frank and candid in his reports to Hitler, and the latter usually agreed with Bock, as long as there was no indication on Bock's part that he was conducting a withdrawal. Hitler was particularly prone to agree with Bock with regard to a tactical reorganization of Army Group South. For example, on 28 January, Bock decided to combine the Seventeenth Army and the First Panzer Army into one organization under the command of Field Marshal Ewald von Kleist, one of Germany's leading experts in armored warfare. His purpose for doing this was to present a stronger front to the Russian attacks in the Isyum-Slavyansk salient south of Kharkhov. When Bock reported to Hitler what he had done, he found Hitler in complete agreement. On another occasion, two days later, Bock reported by telephone to Hitler that fifty new tanks had not arrived in his command, as had been promised. In this particular case, and in later similar cases, Bock circumvented at least half a dozen higher, intermediate agencies in the German Army, even though Hitler was Supreme Commander. But he did this purposely and deliberately, and perhaps with diabolic glee. Seldom did he talk to Halder, who, after von Brauchitsch's removal, was the highest officer at Army High Command. Whenever there was a discussion between Bock and the Army High Command, a verbal altercation usually resulted.[10]

In early February, the Russian attacks slackened, though they did not break off completely. Throughout most of February, Russian cavalry divisions made determined, repeated attempts to cut through the German lines in the Donets salient, but except for "local penetrations" they were generally repulsed by German armor, artillery, and air power.[11] Thus Bock found time to devote attention to preparations for the forthcoming offensive. He hoped to be able to apply the principle of surprise, but this was hardly to be achieved, in view of the Russian's more effective intelligence and better organized partisan activity in the area of Army Group South. Bock was sure that the Russians knew exactly the nature of Hitler's war plans for a grand summer offensive. Already in late January the Russian press and radio had reported that Hitler planned to attack the Caucasus during the coming summer. The British, too, Bock noted, had been profuse with their pronouncements and predictions of the coming offensive.[12]

Yet Bock was inclined to believe, perhaps as a result of his closer contacts with Hitler, that the Russians had been fatally weakened militarily, economically, and politically during the past ten months and that they would not be able to withstand a well-planned, strong German drive in the southern regions of their country. He was gratified that the Rumanians, Hungarians, Bulgarians, Croats, and other nations and ethnic groups of southeastern Europe that were now under German influence, were expending notable efforts to mobilize their economic and military forces in concert with the Germans. Elements of the Italian Eighth Army were beginning to arrive in larger numbers in his command area, and the Spanish government had promised a larger contingent of troops for the summer offensive. More importantly, the German forces had been strengthened with heavier and more durable equipment to withstand the rugged Russian terrain. Another innovation, in particular, was a heavier tank, the Mark IV.[13] Bock began to visualize a new, powerful *Drang nach Osten* (eastern offensive).

By 1 March, Bock had worked out the tactical concept of the offensive. He outlined this in a long letter to Hitler. The concept reflected Bock's traditional, conservative approach to military operations, based upon his many years of professional training and experience. It would be necessary, Bock wrote to Hitler, to secure the army group's southern and northern flanks before undertaking the summer offensive into the Caucasus. To do this, Bock proposed to eliminate Russian forces remaining in the Crimea and Kerch peninsulas, capture Sevastopol, and anchor his southern flank on the Black Sea. To secure the northern flank, he proposed to conquer Voronezh, a city of 300,000 on the Don River, almost 1000 miles north of Sevastopol. Bock believed that in addition to the possibility of achieving flank security, the possibility of achieving an element of surprise also existed. The attack on Voronezh would serve as a feint to draw Russian forces away from the southernmost area and increase chances for a quick breakthrough. The code name for the general offensive would be Operation *Blue*.[14]

As preparatory measures, the Byelgorod-Kharkhov-Isyum salient would have to be eradicated; this operation was scheduled to begin on 1 April and had the code name Operation *Frediricus*. Bock believed *Frediricus* would also serve a twofold purpose, in line with his broader concept of securing the extreme northern and southern flanks of the army group and providing deception. In addition to destroying the Russian forces in the salient, German forces would gain momentum for the difficult task of forcing their way across the wide Don River and gaining freedom of movement east of the Don.[15]

In general, Bock's tactical plans and preparations met with Hitler's approval, though Hitler may have had reservations about the advantages of the Voronezh attack. If he did, this apparently was not made clear to Bock, since the disputes that later ensued over the Voronezh attack had dire consequences for Bock.

Throughout March 1942 the Russians sustained their attacks along the front, particularly around Kharkhov and in the Crimea. These attacks proved to be aggravating for Bock and costly for his forces. He noted that, in some instances, the Russians had changed tactics and were employing small, self-sustaining combat teams of company strength or less, instead of the usual mass assaults by waves of infantry. He knew that the old Bolshevik soldier, Marshal Timoshenko, was commanding the Russian South Front, having been sent there by Stalin during the past October, when Bock's forces were hammering at the gates of Moscow. Bock ascertained, also, from intelligence reports that a number of younger officers were now commanding armies and corps in the Red Army. Bock wondered if this change reflected a shortage of manpower, or if the young officers, being more flexible and quicker to learn from experience, were beginning to influence Russian tactical operations more decisively. He directed his intelligence agencies to further investigate this development and to report their findings.[16]

Bock also noted that guerrilla and partisan activity in the rear areas of Army Group South was becoming much bolder. Dozens of unpleasant incidents were reported daily. Railroad tracks were cut; bridges were demolished; supply convoys were attacked from ambush; buildings occupied by Germans were constantly attacked; hundreds of German officers and men were assassinated in Russian towns, villages, and cities far behind the front lines. In several instances, Bock noted to his chagrin, the partisans had even used light artillery against German rear area troops or their allies, the Rumanians, Hungarians, and Italians.

Bock had never been in accord with many aspects of the German occupational policy in Russia, and when in early March a representative from the Ministry for Eastern Occupied Areas paid a visit, Bock used the opportunity to present his own evaluation of the policy.

"I want to see the Russian population in the occupied areas in a quiet and settled state," Bock commented. "This is not a very difficult task, if one establishes reasonable goals and keeps promises to the Russian people. I am happy to see that agrarian reforms have been introduced in the rear areas, including the practice of individual land ownership. I intend to see that this practice is implemented in my command area."

The representative asked Bock for his opinion regarding the religious issue in the occupied areas.

"The same principle applies here as regards land ownership. Promise the Russian people their religious freedom and hold to the promise. It is to be expected that the political system will be entirely revamped, but it is wise not to deprive the people of their social and cultural traditions and customs. If they are permitted to retain these, they will remain quiet and cooperative. If, however, in spite of these benevolent measures the people rebel against occupation authority, I think that they should be repressed relentlessly."

The occupational official asked Bock if he would express his views in a letter to Dr. Emil Koch, Gauleiter of the Ukraine. Bock declined on the grounds that the implementation of political policies in the occupied areas was outside his province. The official then asked Bock if he would present the same views to Koch, if the latter came to visit him. Bock replied: "Most certainly, but I doubt if that would have the desired effect."[17]

On 1 April, Operation *Frediricus* began. Kleist's huge task force, which Bock had organized several weeks earlier under the name of Army Group Kleist, led the attack. Melting snows and heavy rains made movement difficult; nevertheless, the operation was spectacularly successful, and by mid-April organized Russian military forces had been cleared of the area west of the Don. In the process, the Russians lost 350,000 men, including 200,000 prisoners of war. German losses numbered less than 50,000. The German press dramatically proclaimed the victory, but Bock was not overly impressed. He had learned by now that the Russians possessed remarkable, and very unpredictable, recuperative power.[18]

During the third week of April, Bock flew to Berlin for a week's leave. He spent the time in relaxation, attended the opera, talked with old friends, and consulted his doctors, who told him that his health was better than it had been a year earlier.

Upon his return to Poltava, Bock occupied himself with preparations for the offensive in the Crimea, the first phase of Operation *Blue*. On 28 April, he made an inspection tour of the Crimea and Kerch peninsulas. There he was the guest of Field Marshal Erich von Manstein, commander of the Eleventh Army, with headquarters at Simferopol. He visited a number of subordinate organizations in Eleventh Army, including the XXX Infantry Corps, where he was pleased to see his long-time friend and former chief of staff, von Salmuth. He also visited Air Fleet 4, which was now commanded by another colleague, von Richthofen.[19]

It was Bock's first and only sight of the Russian Crimea, and he was impressed by the beauty of the landscape. "We rode many miles over magnificent mountains and terraced farmlands and along the beautifully serene seashore of the Crimea. It is difficult to reconcile all of this natural beauty with the rigors of warfare," he noted later.[20] The German forces' enormous concentrations of heavy artillery on the inland approaches to Sevastopol reminded Bock, however, that a war was still in progress. With Manstein, Richthofen, Salmuth, and other officers, he went to a forward artillery observation post overlooking Sevastopol, which was scheduled to be conquered as a phase of the great summer offensive. Through a powerful telescope Bock could discern huge signs printed in both German and Russian, which the Russians had erected in front of the fortifications guarding the historic port city. The signs read: "Come ahead, Fascist dogs! We are waiting!" Bock grimly observed that a few well-placed 650-millimeter mortar shells would quickly erase the signs.[21]

Back at his headquarters, Bock reported his impressions to Hitler in a long telephone conversation. Hitler was anxious to know if the attack in the Crimea was scheduled to begin on 8 May, as directed. Bock stated that it was, but again he complained to Hitler of his woes with regard to the transportation system. "The partisans are making it difficult to operate the railroads with any semblance of punctuality," he stated. "Acts of sabotage are increasing at an alarming rate." Hitler dismissed Bock's complaints with the remark that all partisans must be shot without discrimination.[22]

On 8 May, Bock's forces attacked in the Crimea on schedule. Within ten days they had conquered the Kerch Peninsula and had decisively defeated the Russian forces in that area. The conquest of the peninsula and its main city, Kerch, apparently achieved the surprise that Bock had anticipated. The Russians had evidently expected a concentrated assault on Sevastopol and had taken few, if any, precautions for evacuating their forces at Kerch by sea. Consequently, Manstein's Eleventh Army, supported by the Fourth Rumanian Army, quickly pinned the Russians against the seashore. By 18 May, the attack in the Kerch Peninsula had netted over 160,000 prisoners of war and large amounts of heavy artillery and other war supplies. Bock was pleased to report to Hitler that German losses came to only 7000 men.[23]

On 20 May, Bock issued an order stating that 3 June was the commencement date for the attack on Sevastopol. He ordered five days of artillery and air bombardment, to be followed by tank and infantry attacks, beginning on 8 June.

On 1 June, Hitler flew to Poltava under heavy fighter escort to visit Bock. "Considering the fact that the Führer arose at 4:00 A. M. this morning to make the trip here and return in one day, I found him in a surprisingly good mood," Bock noted.[24]

Perhaps one of the reasons for Hitler's jovial mood at Poltava was that the Russians had admitted defeat in the Kerch Peninsula even before the Germans had proclaimed victory. Hitler interpreted this as sound evidence that the Russians were on the verge of complete collapse, and by admitting their losses, they hoped to invoke the help of the Western Powers before it was too late.

"But we will take care of that!" Hitler proclaimed, as he savagely stamped his boot and slapped his thigh. "If the English and the Americans try to land in the Caucasus, we will push them into Siberia, too! There has been much talk by the English and Americans about establishing a second front in the west, but I doubt if they are foolish enough to try that!"

Bock was not so enthusiastic. He reminded Hitler that all reports from his intelligence agencies showed a tremendous concentration of Russian reserve forces in the Don-

Donets basins and in the northern Caucasus. Moreover, the Russians made no secret of the fact that they knew exactly where the German offensive would take place, and what its objectives were. Added to this disconcerting news was the fact that the Russians were beginning to receive considerable amounts of English and American equipment. "We have been successful in southern Russia thus far, but I do not believe the Russians will permit themselves to be surprised again, as they were at Kerch," he said to Hitler. "The fact that they are concentrating reserve forces in exactly those areas where we will attack precludes surprise."

"And what do these reserves consist of?" retorted Hitler, "Stupid cotton-pickers from Kazakhstan, Mongolian half-apes from East Siberia, who will run away at the first rumble of a tank or the roar of a Stuka! I tell you, Bock, we have them by their coattails! The motto is: Attack! And attack again! This time there will be no severe winter weather to save them. We will be sitting in the Caucasus and operating their oilfields long before then!"[25]

Later on the return flight to Germany, Hitler confided to an aide: "I wish Bock would evince more optimism. He is still looking backward to the kind of fighting that we had in 1916. After this war is won, I will certainly retire him. He is simply too old-fashioned to take part in our future plans."[26]

On 3 June, the carefully planned assault on Sevastopol began with a saturation bombardment by German artillery and bombers. On 8 June, German and Rumanian troops began to attack the vast ring of forts, now reduced to rubble, that guarded Sevastopol by land. The fighting was intense, and to Bock it was reminiscent of past engagements at Warsaw, Dunkirk, Brest-Litovsk, Minsk, Bryansk, and Vyasma. The Russians threw every available man into the battle; all had orders to fight to the last breath. They did, defending their city from beneath every stone. But by mid-

June, it was apparent that Sevastopol would soon fall. On 19 June, Bock recorded that Forts "Lenin" and "North" had been taken, and although the Russians were still resisting fiercely, only secondary defense lines remained to be overcome before German troops entered the city and occupied the entire Crimea. Bock noted, also, that the Rumanians were fighting effectively alongside the German forces. "Our military advisers have had trouble with the nonmilitary Rumanians, but the situation is improving," he wrote.[27]

During the Battle of Sevastopol, Bock reported almost daily to Hitler on its progress. Since he had visited Bock, Hitler had spent most of June at his Bavarian retreat, Obersalzberg. Usually at 5:00 P. M., Bock called over the telephone lines that spanned the vast distance between German Bavaria and the Russian Crimea. In one of his last such calls, Bock informed Hitler that Army Group South was prepared to launch the second and all-important phase of Operation *Blue*, the summer offensive into Stalingrad and the Caucasus, on 28 June 1942.

A serious incident now occurred that was to have fateful consequences for Germany, for Army Group South, and for Field Marshal von Bock. On 20 June, a small German courier airplane with the operations officer of the 23rd Panzer Division, Major Anton Reichel, and his pilot aboard, was returning to divisional headquarters from XL Panzer Corps. Reichel was carrying a copy of the operational plans for the German offensive, which was scheduled to begin within the week. The plans were labeled "Top Secret—By Officer Courier Only." The plane encountered a severe spring thunderstorm, the pilot lost direction and the plane strayed off course over Russian-held territory. Whether the plane had mechanical trouble or was hit by Russian anti-aircraft fire has not been fully established. At any rate, the plane crashed in Russian-held territory within about three miles of the German lines, near Byelgorod.

Reichel and the pilot were killed, but the plane did not burn when it crashed. German forward observers reported the crash of the airplane.

The grave possibility that the German war plans had fallen into Russian hands rippled through the command structure of Army Group South like an earthquake. As soon as it became known at the headquarters of the 23rd Panzer Division that the courier airplane had crashed almost within sight of the German lines, the divisional commander acted quickly. He ordered the airplane to be destroyed at all costs, and he reported the incident to his next higher headquarters, XL Panzer Corps. The corps commander reported the event to his commander, Colonel General Friedrich Paulus, commander of the Sixth Army. Paulus called Bock to give him the grave news that efforts to destroy the plane by German sharpshooter fire or by bombing had so far been unsuccessful.[28]

Bock was highly concerned but impassive.

"Recover the plane and the documents as quickly as possible and at all cost," he commanded.[29]

At the 23rd Panzer Division, a hastily organized task force of death-defying German soldiers blasted their way with tanks and self-propelled heavy guns through intense Russian fire to the location of the crashed plane. They recovered the bodies of Major Reichel and his pilot. But the highly classified documents, the German war plans for Operation *Blue* II, were not found. The only assumption that could be made was that Russian soldiers had salvaged the documents.

On 21 June, Army High Command reported the incident regarding the lost documents to Adolf Hitler. The incident prompted Hitler to leave the serenity of his Bavarian Alpine retreat and to return to the Führer's headquarters in East Prussia. On the day of Hitler's arrival, 22 June, Halder recorded in his diary: "Hitler has returned, and once again he is furious with the General Staff. The unfortunate Reichel case seems to be the signal for a complete break between Hitler and the Officer Corps, which has been seething for a long time. Now the dam has really burst. This is not a pleasant way to celebrate the first anniversary of the start of this campaign."[30]

Hitler ordered Bock to report to him immediately. Late on the evening of 24 June, Bock's plane landed at Hitler's headquarters in East Prussia. At 9:00 A. M., 25 June, in accordance with the usual protocol, Bock presented himself to Field Marshal Keitel, preparatory to his conference with Hitler. Keitel was extremely agitated. He demanded to know, first, to what extent German military strategy in Russia had been compromised by the lost secret documents, and, secondly, what punishment did Bock intend to dole out to the officers who were responsible for the grave incident. In answer to the first question, Bock explained that the documents that had apparently fallen into Russian hands contained only the attack orders and military objectives of the XL Panzer Corps and one of its subordinate organizations, the 23rd Panzer Division. It was, therefore, improbable that German military strategy had been compromised to a greater extent in this case than it had been by other means, such as partisan activity, interrogation of high ranking German prisoners, espionage, and interceptions. As far as the punishment of the responsible officers was concerned, Bock stated that he had already severely reprimanded the commanders of the XL Panzer Corps and the 23rd Panzer Division and that was the extent of the punitive action he intended to take. The incident of the crashed airplane, Bock explained further, was unfortunate, but it was of the kind that happened not infrequently in modern military operations.[31]

Keitel became even more agitated. "The Führer," he stated, "is very distressed about this incident. He sees in it just another manifestation of the irresponsibility and incompetence among German officers. The Führer has delegated me to inform you that the incident is a case of outright disobedience, and that he intends to make an example of the offending officers, beginning with you, Field Marshal Bock!"[32]

Bock angrily told Keitel that the latter's attitude and remarks were only another indication that Armed Forces High Command was not aware of the difficulties that faced the German field forces in Russia, that it was demonstrably clear that reports from Army Group South were not read or digested at Armed Forces High Command, and, finally, that Keitel had better have second thoughts before considering punitive action against him.

After this heated exchange Keitel left the room, apparently to consult Hitler. Bock waited for almost an hour in an anteroom, as Hitler, Keitel, and other close associates of Hitler discussed the next move. After an hour, Schmundt appeared and asked if Bock would now see Hitler.

For the first time since the two men had known each other, Hitler did not step forward to greet Bock with outstretched hand. He gave Bock a curt nod and continued to pace agitatedly back and forth. Besides Hitler and Bock, Keitel, Schmundt, and one or two secretaries were present at this conference. Hitler listened without interrupting, as Bock again explained in detail what had happened in the case of the lost documents. Bock concluded with a reference to Keitel's earlier remarks about flagrant disobedience among the officers of the German Army.

"You have no need for concern about this issue," he told Hitler. "As an experienced, professional soldier, I know that there is no foundation for such an accusation. Every high officer in my command, and throughout the entire German Army, acts quickly and decisively to rectify a situation in which there are indications of disobedience or dereliction of duty. Every high officer is capable of punishing offenders."[33]

Bock noted later that Hitler appeared to relax, and listened quietly until Bock had concluded. Hitler then announced that he would make no decision in the case for the moment, which Bock noted "was to be expected," and turned the conversation to a general discussion of the military situation in Army Group South.

"As I took leave of Hitler," Bock recorded, "he was again friendly and appeared to have a different viewpoint than when our discussion began."[34]

Bock returned immediately to his headquarters by special airplane and continued to supervise preparations for the great summer offensive. On 27 June, Bock learned to his astonishment that, according to direct instructions from Hitler, the commanders of the XL Panzer Corps and the 23rd Panzer Division were to be removed from command in disgrace and placed in involuntary retirement. Bock filed the usual protests at Army High Command but they availed nothing. He considered having the dismissed officers brought before him, in order to investigate personally their situations, but he concluded that the pressure of responsibility with regard to conducting the forthcoming attack did not permit sufficient time to resolve the incident.

On 28 June, the great attack began. In bloody, costly fighting, the forces of Army Group South forced their way across the Don and Donets rivers and established bridgeheads in several places. Within a few days it was apparent that the Germans had broken through the Russian front from Kursk to Isyum. On 1 July, a special bulletin from Hitler's headquarters announced the fall of Sevastopol.[35]

On 3 July, Hitler flew to Bock's headquarters. He was accompanied on the trip by Halder and several high officers of Army High Command. It was the second time that Hitler and Bock had met within two weeks.

Bock wrote later:

The Führer was in a jovial mood and was obviously pleased
with the progress of the offensive, and especially with the fall
of Sevastopol and the liquidation of the enemy in the Crimea.
We discussed the supply situation, and I informed him that
there had been noticeable improvement during the past days.
... I broached the subject of attacking Voronezh.... The
Führer authorized me to seize this vital center as a means of
securing my northern flank, but not to expend "needless" effort
in men and time on the Voronezh attack, because the focal
point of the offensive was directed at Stalingrad and the
Caucasus.... He asked me to what extent the lost secret documents were affecting the operation and if the enemy had been
alerted for the attack. I replied that it was difficult to evaluate
that point for the time being.... [36]

On 5 July, two of Bock's divisions entered Voronezh with
surprising ease, but as the divisions fanned out eastward
and northeastward of the city, they came under very heavy
Russian counterattacks. As a result, the Germans found
themselves engaged in a bitter fight, hundreds of miles north
of their main goal, the oilfields of the Caucasus. Bock decided to order two more divisions of the XL Panzer Corps
to Voronezh, to overcome heavy Russian resistance in the
area as rapidly as possible. He estimated that the additional
troops could secure the area within a few days, after which
he would require them to veer southeastward to support the
main attack.

Bock's commitment of additional troops to the Voronezh
area appeared to be, on the surface, a practical operational
matter, dictated by operational necessity. He was intent
upon securing his northern as well as his southern flank before committing the full weight of his enormous forces
against Stalingrad and the Caucasus. He remembered the
dangerous, ever-constant threat that the Russians had posed

on the southern flank of his Army Group Center, as it had approached Moscow during the previous autumn. He did not wish a similar situation to develop in his Army Group South.

Apparently, Bock did not suspect that Hitler would regard his decision to concentrate more troops at Voronezh as anything other than a practical matter. During the past weeks, Hitler had approved *ex post facto* several decisions that Bock had made in similar circumstances such as his reorganization of the armored forces under Kleist and his decision to conquer the Kerch Peninsula. But for reasons that German military records do not clarify, Hitler and the Armed Forces High Command immediately castigated Bock regarding the Voronezh operation and demanded that he withdraw the forces at Voronezh. Remembering that only a few days before, Hitler had approved, in effect, the attack on Voronezh, Bock chose to disregard Hitler's countermanding instructions. This act proved to be Bock's undoing.

As the attack at Voronezh continued, Hitler became more and more furious and openly questioned Bock's ability to conduct the entire operation. Hitler established a line near Voronezh, north of which Bock was forbidden to send troops. During the next days, Bock engaged in a series of long telephone discussions with first Hitler, then Keitel, then Halder, and then back to Hitler.[37]

All were unpleasant and confusing and all seemed to lead to more and more misunderstanding between Bock and Hitler and the officers in Hitler's headquarters, regarding the course that the summer offensive should pursue.

On 7 July, in accordance with plans that had been previously worked out at Armed Forces High Command, Army Group South was dissolved, and in its place were established Army Groups "A" and "B." Bock commanded Army Group "B"; List commanded Army Group "A."

At about noon on 13 July, the telephone rang in Bock's

offices at Poltava. Keitel was on the line, calling from East Prussia for perhaps the twentieth time during the past few days. The following conversation took place:

Keitel: The Führer has directed me to inform you that on 15 July you will give command of Army Group "B" to von Weichs and will return to Germany.

Bock: This is a most astounding development! What is the reason for it?

Keitel: I am only carrying out the Führer's instructions.

Bock: I demand to know the reason for this surprising move.

Keitel: The Führer has directed that you give up your command for reasons of health. Besides, he is very unhappy that you ordered two more divisions to Voronezh, thus impairing the attack farther southward. Also, your supply system is malfunctioning.

Bock: Fuel and supplies are not reaching the combat zone. Until they do, they are not my responsibility. The breakdown of the supply system is occurring in the homeland and far behind the front. As for Voronezh, that issue has been buffeted back and forth too much already. The situation there has been cleared up, and it is purposeless to discuss it further!

Keitel: It serves no purpose, also, if you become so irritated! My duty is difficult enough here, and I do not propose to engage in a useless argument. I do not believe the situation is irreparable. For the moment, it is impossible to discuss this with the Führer; he is far too busy. Later perhaps, but for now, I have no desire to quarrel with you![38]

Upon this unpleasant note ended Field Marshal von Bock's active military career of forty-five years' service to Germany.

Long after the conversation with Keitel ended, Bock sat as if thunderstruck. When he informed his Chief of Staff, Lieutenant General Georg von Sodenstern, and his Operations Officer, Brigadier General August Winter, what had happened, they expressed surprise and astonishment.

An hour or so after talking to Bock, Keitel called again. This time he talked only to Sodenstern and directed him to place Field Marshal von Bock on the German Army's sick list.

On 14 July, Weichs arrived at Poltava to replace Bock. Apparently still unable to fathom his sudden dismissal, Bock conferred at length with Weichs regarding latest developments, ending with a detailed summary of the military situation in Army Group "B." He recorded later that Weichs also failed to comprehend the reasons for Bock's removal. "I would have acted in the same manner if I had been in your place," Weichs stated. "In fact, it is I who should be redressed for the course that the operation is taking—not you!"[39]

On 15 July, Bock turned over his command to Weichs in a brief ceremony and departed by airplane for Berlin. The cordial farewell that Weichs and a few staff officers extended to him did not ease Bock's sadness and bewilderment. He knew that he would never command a German soldier again, but he was determined to maintain his own honor as a soldier.

The next weeks and months witnessed what must be recorded as one of the greatest hoaxes in modern military history. When Adolf Hitler relieved Bock from command, he directed not only that there be no public announcement of the event, but that Bock's dismissal from active command be kept in strictest secrecy throughout the German Army. Hitler and the German military hierarchy were more successful in maintaining secrecy regarding Bock's situation than they were in keeping their secret plans for the summer offensive of 1942 from falling into the hands of the Russians.

In Berlin, Bock was far from satisfied with developments. For several days after his arrival, he attempted unsuccessfully to contact Hitler at his East Prussian headquarters.

In each attempt he received vague replies to the effect that Hitler was not available or that he was absent on official business elsewhere. With absolutely nothing to do, Bock donned civilian clothes and took long walks in the Jung-fernheide sector of Berlin, near his apartment. One evening, after returning from a long stroll, Bock received a caller at his apartment. The caller identified himself as a high official of the *Sicherheitspolizei,* or security police, a branch of Himmler's SS. With grave cordiality and politeness, the official advised Field Marshal von Bock that he should remain indoors until further notice, so as not to be seen and recognized on the streets of Berlin. The official implied succinctly that if von Bock permitted the advice to go unheeded, other and perhaps more unpleasant measures would be taken to ensure compliance.[40]

Bock dismissed the official curtly, but he remained in his apartment during the next weeks. For news of the progress of the war and his former commands on the Russian front, he had access only to the radio and the press. He had no official contacts with the German Armed Forces at all. But the stubborn, proud von Bock did not give up efforts to exonerate himself and to uncover the truth regarding his abrupt dismissal from command. Attempting to arrange an audience with Hitler, he made numerous telephone calls and wrote numerous letters. The telephone calls availed nothing; the letters were not answered. Through his aides-de-camp, who had returned with him to Berlin, Bock acquired copies of the voluminous war records of Army Group South for the period from January to July 1942. For hours he sat alone in his apartment and pored over the records, making marginal notes and using the records as a basis for writing still more letters to the Armed Forces High Command. As the weeks passed, Bock gradually became resigned to the fact that he was in Berlin to stay and that there would be no call, telegram, or letter, inquiring if von

Bock were available to assume command of an army group, as had happened after the Moscow disaster in January 1942.

On 1 September, as news of the attack on Stalingrad resounded from the German radio and press, Bock received an official document from the Armed Forces High Command. It was the first direct communication he had received since his unpleasant conversation with Keitel in July. The document set forth his current status in the German Army in one phrase: "Extended sick leave."[41] Bock's pay as a field marshal continued to be deposited in his Berlin bank.

On 5 September, the edition of the monthly periodical *Das Reich* displayed prominently a photograph of Field Marshal von Bock on its cover. The feature article reported that Bock was heroically leading his brave German soldiers in the assault on the Bolshevik citadel of Stalingrad, many hundreds of miles from the borders of the Fatherland, that German troops under von Bock's gallant leadership had surged across the Don only a few miles from Stalingrad and were now investing the city.[42]

Other German publications featured similar articles throughout September 1942, and the German radio mentioned Bock in all of its incessant special war bulletins. All over the world, the press and other communications media headlined and portrayed von Bock as Germany's vaunted commander who was directing "hammer blows" at Stalingrad and at Russia's oilfields in the Caucasus. In the United States, a leading national weekly featured von Bock on its front cover for the edition of 13 September 1942 and devoted several pages to Bock and his bloody, costly military operations in Southern Russia.[43]

All the while, Bock sat in his apartment, either in idle contemplation or searching for telltale evidence in the war records of his former command, Army Group South, evidence that would prove that he had been right in his many weighty tactical decisions. He recognized the photographs that purportedly showed him to be leading his forces in Southern Russia as those that had been taken in June 1942, when he was actually in command of Army Group South and had stood on the banks of the Don near Voronezh in company with Weichs, Hoth, Paulus, and other high officers. The accounts of his nonexistent military feats in front of Stalingrad gave von Bock an eerie feeling. "It is ghostly," he wrote. "It is like reading one's own obituary."[44]

Disregarding the probability that his telephone had been tapped, Bock called old friends and military colleagues in Berlin and elsewhere in Germany to elicit their impressions of what was happening in his case. On one occasion, he talked to an old acquaintance, Field Marshal Werner von Blomberg, the former Minister of War of the Third Reich who had been dismissed by Hitler in early 1938. Blomberg, like others, sympathized with Bock, but he was guarded and vague in his comments and offered no helpful suggestions.

Dejected and embittered, Bock confided to his diary: "There is no alternative but to face the fact that I have been made a monstrous scapegoat. What a shame that my beloved Germany must be reduced to such trickery!"[45]

In October 1942, the British press, apparently growing suspicious of the Bock case, published a notice that Bock had been dismissed from command after an argument with Hitler over the strategy and tactics of the Russian campaign. The article compared Bock's dismissal to Ludendorff's in 1918 and stated that this signified the beginning of the end for Germany's military power. The German press quickly and vehemently denied the validity of the British article and stated that Hitler and Bock had never been on better terms.[46]

Soon after the British newspaper article was published, a series of reports concerning von Bock appeared in the foreign press around the world. One report stated that he had been shot; another stated that he had been arrested and was now in a concentration camp; still others noted that he had been seen strolling along the streets of Berlin, Hamburg, and Stettin. In early November, a Swiss newspaper stated that Bock had gone to Japan.[47]

On 3 December 1942, Field Marshal von Bock's sixty-second birthday, he received, among others, a telegram of good wishes signed personally by Adolf Hitler.[48]

Throughout the winter of 1942–43, Bock watched in helpless horror from Berlin, as the proud, once mighty German Army went down to disastrous defeat at Stalingrad. Following the Stalingrad debacle, Germany proclaimed total war, and stated that all able-bodied men up to the age of sixty-five were liable for military service.

"And here I sat, twiddling my thumbs," Bock wrote.[49]

In early 1943, a number of officers with whom Bock had been acquainted during his long military career gradually began to contact him, either by telephone or by personal calls. Some of the officers talked and acted surreptitiously; others were more outspoken. The most notable of the officers was Colonel General Ludwig Beck, former Chief of the General Staff. Beck expressed the firm opinion that Germany could no longer win the war. Consequently, would Bock join him and other officers in a movement to bring hostilities to a halt? Bock considered the matter carefully but declined on the basis that such activity constituted high treason and that it could probably lead to civil war, which would hasten Germany's destruction.[50]

The Third Reich celebrated Memorial Day on 21 March. For the celebration the Armed Forces High Command planned an exposition to be held in Berlin. The exposition included a display of the latest German arms and equipment, as well as captured Russian military items of every imaginable description. A few days before the exposition, Bock received an invitation from Armed Forces High Command to attend its formal opening. The invitation was the second direct communication that he had received since the past July. After some deliberation Bock decided to accept.

Adolf Hitler appeared at the exposition and gave a short address. Bock attended a reception that followed, and he and Hitler exchanged cool greetings and brief handshakes. Bock wore his marshal's uniform for the first time since he had 'returned to Berlin. He remained in Hitler's presence for several minutes, tall, erect, and towering over Hitler and the immediate members of his entourage. Bock noticed that Hitler had aged considerably since they had last met in early July 1942 in the Russian Ukraine. Hitler was more withdrawn, nervous, and ill at ease. After a few preliminary remarks about Germany's general military situation, Bock attempted to bring up the subject of his own status with Hitler. He informed Hitler that he stood ready, as always, to render service to Germany and asked if the possibility existed that he might be recalled to active duty and to lead Germany's soldiers in the difficult days ahead.[51]

Hitler did not answer Bock directly and indicated both by his manner and a few curt remarks that he did not intend to discuss Bock's status. Shortly afterward, Hitler left the exposition, accompanied by *Reichsmarschall* Hermann Göring, Keitel, Reich Minister of the Interior Wilhelm Frick, and other officials. The occasion marked the last time that Adolf Hitler and Fedor von Bock met face to face.

Except for a few brief visits to his old family estate at Küstrin, Bock spent the remainder of 1943 in Berlin. In the fall of that year, his Berlin apartment was damaged by Allied bombs, but after having the most extensive damage repaired, Bock and his family continued to reside in it. By now he was receiving frequent letters and calls from various military and civil officials, some of whom Bock did not know, asking when would he return to active duty as a field commander, for Germany's hour of fate was nearing and Germany needed strong-hearted, professional soldiers to save her. Bock answered a few of these with the statement that his services to Germany were apparently not required by her leaders. In several instances, he received anonymous letters accusing him of having led Germany to disaster at Moscow and thus paving the road for her final defeat.[52]

In the spring of 1944, as the Allied bombardment of Berlin steadily increased, Bock decided to move to another ancient family land holding in Grodtken, East Prussia. He remained there until the end of the year, when the Red Army's offensive forced millions of Germans to evacuate East Prussia.

Bock's reaction to the final attempt to assassinate Hitler in July 1944 was phlegmatic. "Do they not see that they are only destroying themselves; that this is not the way to save Germany?" he wrote. But Bock apparently had no alternative for the salvation of Germany. Although Bock was aware of the existence of an anti-Hitler conspiracy, it is certain that he took no active part in the events of July 1944. In early August, Colonel von Hardenberg, Bock's former aide-de-camp, was executed for his part in the Hitler plot. Bock had left Hardenberg in Berlin during the past spring. His reaction to Hardenberg's execution was sharper than it had been to the attempted assassination of Hitler. From his East Prussian home, he contacted the grief-stricken Frau von Hardenberg and invited her to stay with him and his family.[53] Frau von Hardenberg decided not to accept the invitation. If she had, it is possible that the German secret police may have regarded Bock with suspicion of complicity in the plot.

On 3 December 1944, Bock's sixty-fourth birthday, a telegram expressing best birthday wishes arrived from Adolf Hitler. It was the last communication between the two men. Bock accepted the birthday wishes laconically and did not bother to reply.[54]

In early 1945, with the fortunes of war inexorably worsening for Germany, Bock left East Prussia and stayed for a while in Kolberg, a Prussian town on the Baltic Sea. By March 1945, Russian onslaughts had forced him to move to Pritzwalk, about eighty miles north of Berlin. Germany was rapidly becoming exhausted, as the Russians, Americans, British, and French pressed their attacks from east and west.

On 28 April 1945, Field Marshal von Bock received a telegram from a former colleague and subordinate, Field Marshal von Manstein. The telegram had been delayed for several days, because of the complete collapse of Germany's communications and transportation systems. The telegram requested Bock to come, if conditions permitted, to Hamburg, where under the jurisdiction of Admiral of the Fleet Karl Dönitz a "North German" government was being formed. Bock was not sure what purpose such a government could serve at this late hour. But he decided to attempt the trip, even though chaotic conditions that now reigned over the length and breadth of Germany made safe travel a very unlikely prospect. He prepared to leave on the following morning.

On 30 April, while attempting to reach Hamburg by automobile, Bock learned that Hitler was dead. On 2 May, Bock and his driver reached Schwarzenbek, near Hamburg, having been harried every yard of the way by Allied bombers and fighters, which by now ranged at will over the German countryside, bombing and strafing every object that moved. At Schwarzenbek, Bock was advised by police not to proceed, because British troops had entered Hamburg from the west. Bock decided to drive around Hamburg and, if possible, reach Kiel. But, in reality, he could see no earthly reason for trying to contact Manstein or Dönitz. There was simply no more hope.

"What can we do now? The end is approaching with giant steps," was Bock's last written statement.[55]

On 7 May 1945, amid glowing reports of Nazi Germany's impending surrender, a news dispatch appeared in several leading American and British newspapers: "The riddled body of General Field Marshal Fedor von Bock was found by British troops north of Hamburg yesterday. He had been dead for several days and may have been caught in a strafing raid. . . . Von Bock's body either had been ignored or not recognized by German troops and had been left for a burial squad to pick up. . . ."[56]

It was an inglorious end for an old soldier.

1. Von Bock KTB, 3 January 1942. 2. *Ibid.*, 6 January 1942. 3. 16 January 1942. 4. 17 January 1942.

5. *Der Völkische Beobachter*, 8 January 1942.

6. Von Bock KTB, 18 January 1942.

7. Tippelskirch, pp. 210ff. The Italian Eighth and Rumanian Fourth Armies comprised the greater combat strength of Germany's allied forces in Southern Russia.

8. Zentner, p. 28.

9. Von Bock KTB, 21 January 1942.

10. H. Gp. Süd KTB, microfilm no. 273/55479/2/670–81 (Washington, D.C.: U.S. National Archives, n.d.).

11. *Ibid.*, microfilm no. 273/55479/2/698–705.

12. John Armstrong and Kurt De Witt, "Organization and Control of the Partisan Movement" (Washington, D.C.: Air Research and Development Command, U.S. Air Force, 1954), pp. 13–48. See also Von Bock KTB, 1–10 February 1942.

13. H. Gp. Süd KTB, microfilm no. 273/55479/2/711 (Washington, D.C.: U.S. National Archives, n.d.).

14. *Ibid.*, microfilm no. 273/55479/2/734–48. 15. *Ibid.*

16. Von Bock KTB, 1–23 March 1942. 17. *Ibid.* 18. 18 April 1942.

19. *Ibid.*, 28–29 April 1942. 20. 2 May 1942. 21. *Ibid.* 22. 3 May 1942. 23. 19 May 1942. See also Tippelskirch, pp. 274–78.

24. Von Bock KTB, 1 June 1942. 25. *Ibid.*

26. Germany, 1952. Personal interview with a confidential source. Hitler's remark was alledgedly made to Jodl, who accompanied him to Poltava, and was overheard by a junior aide-de-camp.

27. Von Bock KTB, 19 June 1942.

28. Friedrich Paulus, *Ich Stehe hier auf Befehl* (Berlin, 1955), pp. 182ff; *Kriegstagebuch des Oberkommandos der Wehrmacht*, vol. II (Frankfurt, 1965), p. 445; H. Gp. Süd KTB, microfilm no. 297/75124/1/382 (Washington, D.C.: U.S. National Archives, n.d.); and Halder KTB, III, 20 June 1942, p. 460.

29. Von Bock KTB, 20 June 1942. See also Halder KTB, III, 22 June 1942, p. 464. The name of the pilot is not recorded.

30. Halder KTB, III, 23 June 1942, p. 466.

31. Von Bock KTB, 25 June 1942. 32. *Ibid.* 33. *Ibid.* 34. *Ibid.*

35. H. Gp. Süd KTB, microfilm no. 273/55479/2/841 (Washington, D.C.: U.S. National Archives, n.d.).

36. Von Bock KTB, 3 July 1942.

37. *Ibid.*, 7 July 1942. Halder sided with Hitler and remarked that Bock must have suffered a lapse when he made this "nonsensical" decision. See Halder KTB, III, 7–10 July 1942, pp. 475–77.

38. Von Bock KTB, 13 July 1942. 39. *Ibid.*, 14 July 1942.

40. Germany, 1951. Personal interview with a former official of the Nazi German secret police.

41. Von Bock KTB, 2 September 1942.

42. *Das Reich*, 5 September 1942.

43. *Time*, 13 September 1942.

44. Von Bock KTB, 17 September 1942. 45. *Ibid.*, 28 September 1942. 46. 3 October 1942.

47. Bock noted in his diary that the Swiss newspaper report emanated from Zurich, but he did not identify the newspaper. See Von Bock KTB, 3 November 1942.

48. *Ibid.*, 3 December 1942. 49. 1 February 1943.

50. *Ibid.*, 19 February 1943. Beck was implicated in the July 1944 plot to assassinate Hitler and committed suicide. See Wheeler-Bennett, p. 397.

51. Von Bock KTB, 22 March 1943. 52. 1–31 October 1943. 53. 23 July and 5 August 1944.

54. *Ibid.*, 3 December 1944. 55. 3 May 1945.

56. *New York Times*, 7 May 1945.

ILLUSTRATIONS

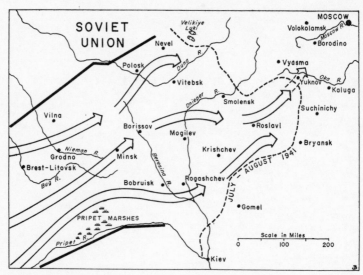

Army Group Center's Advance, July - August 1941

Command structure of Army Group Center at Beginning of German-Russian Campaign, June 1941

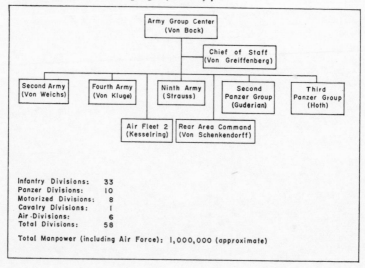

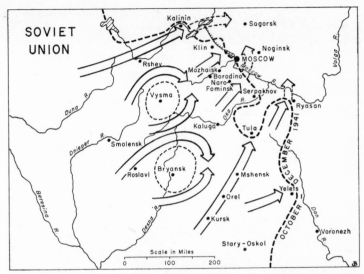

Battle of Moscow, October - December 1941

Command structure of Army Group Center in Battle of
Moscow, October - December 1941

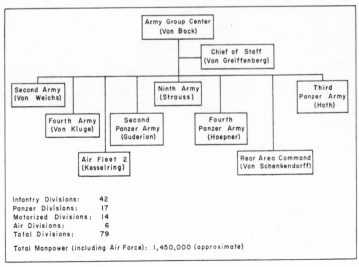

Infantry Divisions: 42
Panzer Divisions: 17
Motorized Divisions: 14
Air Divisions: 6
Total Divisions: 79

Total Manpower (including Air Force): 1,450,000 (approximate)

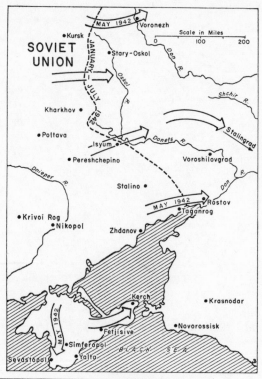

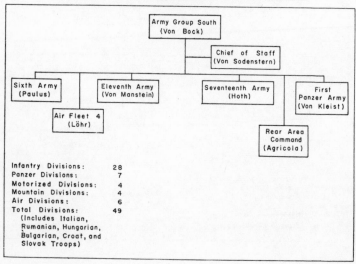

Infantry Divisions: 28
Panzer Divisions: 7
Motorized Divisions: 4
Mountain Divisions: 4
Air Divisions: 6
Total Divisions: 49
   (Includes Italian,
   Rumanian, Hungarian,
   Bulgarian, Croat, and
   Slovak Troops)

Opposite, above: Army Group South's advance, January-
July 1942

Opposite, below: Command structure of Army Group South,
January-July 1942

Below: Eastern Europe, 1941

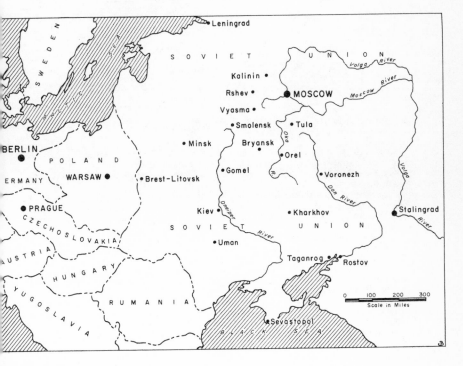

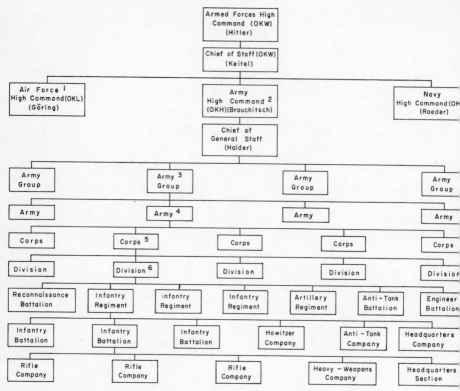

Organization of German Armed Forces, 1941-42

[1] Although the air force was a separate, independent organization, its field units came under the control of the senior army officer in the operational area.

[2] In December 1941 Hitler assumed direct command of the army and, in effect, dissolved this office.

[3] An army group was the largest field organization under the command of a single officer, usually a field marshal. Its structure was both flexible and complex. In 1941-42 an army group consisted of two to four armies, a rear area command, and supporting air force units.

[4] An army had two to five corps. At the beginning of the Russian campaign only the ordinary, or infantry, army existed. Later the armored groups became armored armies. An army was commanded usually by a colonel general.

[5] A corps had two to five divisions. There were several types of corps; in 1941-42 the infantry and the armored corps were the most prominent. The commander of a corps was usually a lieutenant general.

[6] Organization of an infantry or grenadier division. Armored, motorized, mountain, airborne, and other types of divisions were similar in structure but differed greatly in composition. The manpower in a division also varied, ranging from 10,000 men in a mountain division to 17,000 men in an infantry division. Two to seven divisions made up a corps. The division commander was a major general.

Von Bock reviews troops

Hitler congratulates von Bock on 60th birthday

Von Bock takes salute

German tanks on Russian plains

Poor roads test man and machines

Below: Devastation at Vyasma and Bryansk

Opposite, above: Styr River bridge after destruction

Opposite, below: Russian woman flees desolated town

Opposite, above: Battle - strained German faces

Opposite, below: Faces of the conquered

Below: Russian prisoners

German troops advance through Russian village

Snow impedes German drive to Moscow

UNPUBLISHED GERMAN MILITARY RECORDS
form the core of the bibliography used in this study. Since these
voluminous records have not been translated into English, the original
German titles are used. Other sources include contemporary English
and German periodicals, journals, newspapers, and this writer's private collection of memoranda. General histories of the Second World
War and the German campaigns in Russia have not been used ex-
tensively. Only those general works that cite Field Marshal von Bock
specifically or refer to the military organizations he commanded are
listed.

UNPUBLISHED SOURCES

Bock, Fedor von. *Generalfeldmarschall von Bock Kriegstagebuch:
Mai 1939–Mai 1945*, Microfilm No. T-84. Washington, D.C.: U.S.
National Archives, n.d.

Field Marshal von Bock maintained a personal war diary from May
1939 to the day before his death in May 1945. The diary contains over
1000 typewritten pages of entries and has been indispensable to this
study. In some cases, they contain lengthy, detailed, highly technical
remarks concerning the military campaigns that von Bock directed,
as well as his own evaluation of the campaigns. In 1952 the Chief of
Military History, European Command, U.S. Army, purchased the
original diary from von Bock's daughter, Mrs. Ursula von Kreisler.
Subsequently the U.S. National Archives reproduced the diary on
microfilm and returned the original document to West Germany for
deposit in the archives of the German Federal Republic. A microfilm
copy is in this writer's possession.

*Kriegstagebücher der Heeresgruppen Mitte und Süd mit Anlagen,
Beurteilungen, Aufmarschanweisungen, Skizzen, Kräftegliederungen
und sonstigen Niederschriften von April 1941 bis Juli 1942*, microfilm
nos. 215, 216, 220, 221, 226, 233, 273, 288, and 289. Washington, D.C.:
U.S. National Archives, n.d.

These unpublished military records numbering approximately 20,000
typewritten pages, are a part of the vast quantities of German official
documents that came into possession of the United States Government
at the end of the Second World War. They are extremely valuable in
a study of Field Marshal von Bock and the German campaigns in
Russia. During the past decade the U.S. National Archives has re-

produced these records on microfilm and has returned the original documents to the German Federal Republic. For the most part the records are reproduced at random and without regard to subject or chronological order. References in this study are made by microfilm roll number, item number, and microfilm frame number, in accordance with catalog, "Guides to German Records Microfilmed at Alexandria, Virginia," No. 52, U.S. National Archives, Washington, D.C., 1966. The microfilm listed in this study is now the property of the University of New Mexico, Albuquerque.

Armstrong, John, and DeWitt, Kurt. "Organization and Control of the Partisan Movement." Washington, D.C.: U.S. Air Force, Air Research and Development Command, Human Resources and Research Institute, Maxwell Air Force Base, Alabama, 1954.

Ziemke, Earl. "The Soviet Partisan Movement in 1941." New York: Air Research and Development Command, Human Resources Research Institute, Maxwell Air Force Base, Alabama, U.S. Air Force, Washington, D.C., 1954. Published at Columbia University by contractual agreement with the U.S. Air Force.
The articles provide detailed, authoritative information about Soviet partisan warfare during the German campaigns.

PERSONAL SOURCES

Germany: Personal interviews with former members of the German Wehrmacht: 1946–62.
This writer conducted these unofficial interviews while stationed in Germany as a U.S. Army intelligence officer. The persons named here were for the most part unaware that their comments would later contribute to this study. This does not, however, detract from the value of their comments, since they either knew Field Marshal von Bock personally or were subordinate to his military commands. The present whereabouts of many of these persons are unknown, though some are known to be deceased. This writer herewith acknowledges the information provided by the following:
Colonel General Heinz Guderian (see Published Sources).
Lieutenant General Anton Freiherr von Bechtolsheim (artillery commander and staff officer in Army Group Center; for several years after the war General von Bechtolsheim was a lecturer on military history).
Major General Dr. Hans Speidel (author of *Invasion: 1944;* from 1959–62 General Speidel was commander of Central Forces, Europe, NATO).

Major General Anton Grasser (former motorized division commander in Army Group Center).

Major General Paul Deichmann (former staff officer in Air Fleet 2 on the Russian front in 1941–42).

Police General Kurt Voigt (former unit commander and staff officer in Army Group Center; after the war General Voigt was commander of Central Command, Federal Border Police).

Major General Helmuth von Sanne

Major General Karl von Stamm

Brigadier General Oskar Munzel (staff officer in General Guderian's Second Panzer Army in 1941; after the war General Munzel became commandant of the West German Army's Armored School).

Lieutenant General Otto Guckenberger (former commander of a police division on the Russian front under von Bock's command, later the chief of police of a large Bavarian city).

Colonel Alexander Martin	Master Sergeant Walter von Krüger
Colonel Rudolf Hilgert	Technical Sergeant Frank Lindhagen
Lieutenant Colonel Otto Greiner	Sergeant Karl Bergmann
Lieutenant Colonel Hans Becker	Johann Ertelt
Lieutenant Colonel Karl-Heinz Bernsdorff	Max Bischelsrieder
	Dr. Isaak Livitsky, professor
Captain Hans Krannefeld	Josef Gessner
Captain Peter Mosier	Mrs. Katherine von Hahn

PUBLISHED SOURCES

Bayles, William. "General von Bock." *American Mercury,* vol. LV, no. 233, New York, August 1941.
A short biographical sketch, relating some aspects of Bock's early life.

Carell, Paul. *Hitler Moves East: 1941–1943,* Boston: Little, Brown and Co., 1963. As *Hitler's War on Russia,* London: George G. Harrap & Co. Ltd., 1964.
Translated from the German edition, *Unternehmen Barbarossa.* A comprehensive narrative, giving background on German strategy.

Current Biography. New York, 1942.
A very brief biographical sketch of von Bock.

Das Reich. Berlin, 1942.
Official German military journal published during the Nazi period.

Der Völkische Beobachter. Berlin, 1941–42.
Official newspaper of German National Socialist Party.

Deutscher Beamten-Kalender: 1941. Berlin: Verlag Beamtenpresse Gmbh, 1942.
Annual German almanac, containing official facts and figures.

Gilbert, Felix. *Hitler Directs His War.* New York: Oxford University Press, 1950.
Informative narrative about Hitler and his relationship with the German military hierarchy.

Greiner, Helmuth. *Die Oberste Wehrmachtsführung: 1939-1943.* Wiesbaden, Limes Verlag, 1950.
An account of the intricacies of the German high military leadership in the war's first years.

Guderian, Heinz. *Erinnerungen eines Soldaten.* Heidelberg: Kurt Vornwinckel Verlag, 1951.
One of the first autobiographies by a German general after the Second World War. Provides firsthand, often controversial information on development of the German armored corps between the wars, the concept of the blitzkrieg, and Guderian's relations with Hitler and his superior officers, including von Bock. The English edition of this volume, entitled *Panzer Leader,* was for several years on the recommended professional reading list for officers of the U.S. Army.

Hofe, Werner von. *Der Weg zum Reich.* Berlin: E. Mittler & Sohn, 1944.
A very biased account of Hitler's rise to power and Germany's early victories in the campaign in Russia. Used as a high school text during last years of the Nazi German period.

Hubatsch, Walther. *Hitlers Weisungen für die Kriegsführung.* Stuttgart: W. Kohlhammer Verlag, 1963.
Comprehensive interpretation of Hitler's war directives and their effects upon the military operations.

Jacobsen, Hans-Adolf (ed). *Generaloberst Halder Kriegstagebuch,* vols. II and III. Stuttgart: W. Kohlhammer Verlag, 1963.
Vol. II of Halder's diary covers the period from the fall of France in 1940 to the opening of the German campaign in Russia; vol. III covers the period from the German invasion in June 1941 to Halder's dismissal as Chief of the General Staff in September 1942. An extremely valuable work in a study of von Bock.

Kesselring, Albert. *A Soldier's Record.* New York: Morrow, Inc., 1954. As *The Memoirs of Field-Marshal Kesselring,* London: William Kimber & Co. Ltd., 1953.

Kriegstagebuch des Oberkommandos der Wehrmacht, vol. I. Frankfurt: Bernard and Graefe, 1965.
This huge multivolume work contains daily entries of the German Armed Forces High Command throughout the war. Innumerable references are made to Army Groups Center and South; very few to von Bock himself.

Liddell Hart, B. H. *The German Generals Talk.* New York: Morrow, Inc., 1948. As *The Other Side of the Hill,* London: Cassell & Co. Ltd., 1948, 1951. The 1951 edition is an enlarged version.
This fine work by an eminent military historian provides a character analysis of several high German officers who knew von Bock.

New York Times. New York, 1941–45.

Paulus, Friedrich. *Ich Stehe hier auf Befehl.* Frankfurt: Bernard & Graefe, 1960.
A personal account of the 1942 summer offensive by the German general who surrendered the remnants of the German and Rumanian forces at Stalingrad. Describes relationship with von Bock during early phases of the offensive.

Platanov, S. P.; Pavlenko, N. G.; and Parotkin, I. V. (eds.). *Vtoraya Miravaya Voina,* vol. I. Moscow: Voenniye Isdvo NAVK, 1958.
This two-volume work presents the Russian viewpoint of the German invasion. Vol. I emphasizes the success of the Russian counterattack at Moscow in December 1941.

Pravda. Moscow, 1941. Official newspaper of the Russian Communist Party.

Samsonov, A. M. *Velikaya Bitva pod Moskvoi.* Moscow: Voenniye Isdvo NAVK, 1958.
Describes with considerable candor Bock's attack on Moscow in fall of 1941. The author concedes that the German forces were on the verge of success; he stresses, however, that not the severe winter but superior Russian military tactics were the major cause of the German failure.

Schlabrendorff, Fabian von. *Offiziere gegen Hitler.* Zurich: Europa Verlag, 1946.
Mentions but does not explain von Bock's refusal to participate in conspiratorial plots against Hitler.

Taylor, Telford. *Sword and Swastika.* New York: Simon & Schuster, 1952; London: Victor Gollancz Ltd., 1953.

Very comprehensive study of German Officer Corps during the years preceding the Second World War. Charts showing ranks and seniority of high officers are especially useful.

Time. New York, 8 December 1941 and 13 September 1942.

Tippelskirch, Kurt von. *Geschichte des Zweiten Weltkrieges*. Bonn: Athenäum Verlag, 1951.
Probably the first general history of the Second World War from the German viewpoint to be published after the war. Comprehensive, fairly objective, plentifully supplied with maps and sketches of the campaigns in Russia.

Trevor-Roper, H. R. *Hitler's War Directives: 1939–1945*. London: Macmillan, 1964.
English edition by a prominent historian of Hitler's conduct of the war, with emphasis on the effects of Hitler's war directives on the German military opèrations.

Warlimont, Walter. *Im Hauptquartier der deutschen Wehrmacht: 1939–1945*. Frankfurt: Athenäum Verlag, 1962.
A firsthand account of the conflict and confusion existing in the headquarters of the German Armed Forces High Command, especially after 1941.

Wheeler-Bennett, John W. *The Nemesis of Power: The German Army in Politics—1918–1945*. London: Macmillan & Co. Ltd., 1953; New York: St. Martin's Press, 1954.
This work probably remains to this date the most penetrating analysis of the German military establishment as a state within a state. Contains little about German military operations but is very valuable to a study of the military hierarchy, the relations between the German generals and the Weimar Republic and between them and Hitler, and the role of the generals in the conspiracies against Hitler. Contains revealing passages regarding von Bock.

Zentner, Kurt. *Lehren und Bilder aus dem Russlandfeldzug: 1941–1945*. Hamburg: Grüner Verlag, 1952.
A pictorial, but with revealing commentary.

Zimmermann, Erich, and Jacobsen, Hans-Adolf (eds.). *Deutsche gegen Hitler*. Frankfurt: Bernard & Graefe, 1964.
Brief mention of Bock's refusal to engage in anti-Hitler conspiracy after 1941.

INDEX